Wh
g
about
the
good
news?

what's good about the good news?

The Plan of Salvation in a New Light

---

by Neal Punt

NORTHLAND PRESS

P.O. Box 42756
Chicago, Illinois 60642

CONTENTS

v

Fact #3 - Those who will be finally lost are those and only those, who, in addition to their sin in Adam, throughout their entire life willfully reject or remain indifferent to whatever revelation God has given of himself to them.

The so-called "universalistic" texts are not universal statements. They are generalizations, that is, they are universal declarations that have known exceptions.

Most Christians consider premise A (Chapter One, above) to be the over-all message of the Bible. However, the three biblical **facts** referred to in Chapters Two, Three and Four (above) may not be ignored. These three facts compel us to adopt a new point of view (mind-set), namely, premise B.

All elect persons are certain to come to salvation. All persons are elect in Christ except those who throughout their entire life choose to reject or remain indifferent to God's will as it has been made known to them.

There are not two gospels—one for church people and one for the unchurched and unreached. The promise of the gospel, together with the command to repent and believe, must be announced and declared without differentiating or discriminating to all nations and to all people.

It is the very nature of "news" that it cannot be declared and announced conditionally. The "good news," however, requires a **response** of repentance, faith and joyful obedience. The good news of what God has done for us in Christ as well as all of the gospel's ethical demands (including the demands to repent, believe and obey) are based on the assumption that the hearer has a new standing with God in Christ. These demands are not conditions, prerequisites or prescriptions for attaining a new standing with God.

True faith is a result or fruit of salvation, not a cause, prerequisite or condition for salvation. Faith (as well as repentance and obedience) is absolutely necessary for all who hear the gospel because those who choose to remain indifferent or refuse to repent, believe and live in joyful obedience thereby reject God's will as he has made it known to them.

All persons are elect in Christ except those who, in addition to their sin in Adam, choose to reject or remain indifferent to whatever revelation God has given to them. Therefore, all who die before they can make such a self-determined choice are saved.

Having been created in the likeness of God who does all things for his own glory, all persons have a deep need for recognition from others and a hunger for self-esteem. Premise B (Chapter One) provides a biblical basis for so communicating the gospel that it will engender a positive self-image in those who hear it.

Because God is a law unto himself we may not doubt that he is able apart from the preaching of the Word, to save whom he will. Premise B allows for the possibility that some who live their entire life beyond the reach of the gospel may be saved by the grace of God in Christ.

The premise developed in this book relates to questions that arise in the minds of thoughtful Christians. Among these are the questions of whether few or many will be saved and assurance of salvation.

Both the realization of what may happen if the gospel is not proclaimed and the blessing and joy that come through proclamation of the gospel provide incentives to carry out the Great Commission as commanded by Christ.

The message of missions is not "Christ died for you if you believe in him." The **good news** is "Christ died for you and therefore you must believe in him."

This addendum demonstrates that the premise developed in this book is consistent with the doctrine of the covenant which is the basis for the practice of baptizing infants.

These Seven Couplets are an attempt at bridgebuilding between Arminians and Calvinists. These couplets are consistent with the biblical insights provided by the premise of this book.

Foreword

SEVERAL years ago a beloved Christian brother, who had served the church for many years in various capacities, asked me very earnestly, "What's good about the Good News?" His was a serious question, and he asked it, not because he had studied the Bible so little, but because he was studying it so much. Despite all the evangelism, teaching and preaching that my friend both heard and often did, he was nevertheless troubled by a vague suspicion that something was missing.

Is the Good News of the Gospel the word that God loves *all* sinners and has provided *theoretically* for their salvation if *they* only will respond by an appropriate personal decision for Christ? Non-Calvinist Christians (whom Calvinists label as Arminians, a term many so labeled also use for the sake of clarity) generally say that it is.

"But what if nobody should respond?" the Calvinists ask. "If the salvation announced in the Gospel is merely theoretical and not actually accomplished, doesn't the outcome depend finally on sinners? What's *good* about that kind of Good News?"

This is a two-edged sword. Is the Good News of the Gospel the word that God loves *some* sinners and has actually *accomplished* their salvation, but has passed over others so that they *cannot* possibly be saved no matter what they might think about it? That is Calvinism's Gospel—as most Arminians hear it, and as at least some Calvinists have been frank to admit. "What's *good* about that kind of Good News?" the Arminian echoes back.

Some will simply shrug their shoulders, declare that we cannot solve riddles which have perplexed giants before whom we are

ix

grasshoppers, and contentedly parrot the particular view they themselves were taught —on both sides of the fence.

Others, however, refuse to be satisfied so easily. They feel that
devotion to Scripture requires them to press on for clearer understanding. They are not at all sure that, since God's Word is truth,
those who are committed to it and to each other, are doomed forever
to remain so far apart in understanding.

Right or wrong, I belong in that category. Reared and educated
in the "Arminian" Churches of Christ, I found myself a minority
of one while attending Covenant Theological Seminary. There,
obviously devout Christian scholars challenged me in many ways.
I determined to take seriously every "proof text" they offered.
"Those Scriptures all say something," I reasoned. "It will not do
for me simply to deny the Calvinistic interpretation unless I can
offer another explanation that is at least equally probable in
context."

During the subsequent years, I found myself gradually "Reform-
ing," though not enough to please some Calvinistic friends. The
truth is, I came under suspicion on both sides! But I am not sorry,
even for that, for I am convinced more than ever that the full truth
of Scripture on these subjects is yet to be explicated.

In 1980 I discovered Neal Punt's exciting new book titled
Unconditional Good News, (Wm. B. Eerdmans Publishing Co.,
1980). His notion that all are saved in Christ except those of whom
the Bible says they will be finally lost is disarmingly simple yet
unfathomably profound. More than that, it seemed to provide a
meeting place for good-hearted and knowledgeable Calvinists and
Arminians to seek common understanding, a task which had occu-
pied high priority in my own thinking and work since Covenant
Seminary days a decade before.

I was writing a biblical and historical study of the doctrine of
final punishment at the time, which was eventually published as
The Fire That Consumes, and was grappling with the error of
universalism. Punt's thesis dovetailed with my own conclusions
in that study, and I happily recommended his book in a footnote
to my readers.

Now, in this new book, Neal Punt draws from his work in
Unconditional Good News, as well as from his ongoing study and
dialogue, as he offers his exciting thesis to a broader, popular
audience. No thoughtful reader is likely to agree fully with any

book as stimulating and provocative as this one. But Neal Punt probably will not mind. He is far more interested in stirring up fresh thought than in eliciting sleepy "Amens."

If reading this book makes you respond, "But something more needs to be said," Punt will say "Amen." And challenge you to say it!

Edward Fudge

Preface

THE picture that emerges in this book has been painted with a broad brush. This is the only way the premise developed on these pages can be portrayed. Some claims are made for which the reader will not find adequate support in this volume. This is not an oversight. It is owing to the fact that the thesis developed in this volume has so many facets that it would be easy to get lost in the details.

In an earlier book *Unconditional Good News*, (Wm. B. Eerdmans Publishing Co., 1980) I compared some of the classical exegesis done by many Christian scholars over hundreds of years. From their labors a pattern of the over-all message of God's Word begins to emerge. Those interested in the details can consult that work. In this volume I place before the reader in broad outline what I perceive to be the over-all message of the Bible.

In the above mentioned book I admit that I am not satisfied with the treatment of the so-called "universalistic" texts by Calvinists. I have been amazed at the number of knowledgeable Arminians and Calvinists (denominational leaders, professors, authors, pastors and others) who have responded by admitting that they have never been comfortable with the interpretation of these passages provided by their respective theological traditions.

If the perspective developed in this book has validity, it will take the Christian community many years to fill in and work out all the details of what is suggested. My hope is that the reader will carefully examine what is written and in so doing find encouragement and joy in what I think is a legitimate and God-glorifying way of understanding the good news of salvation.

PREFACE

The reader may find it helpful from time to time to review the table of contents in this volume. The chapter summaries found there will enable the reader to see the general pattern as well as some of the implications of the premise developed in this book.

I owe a word of sincere appreciation to pastors of many different denominations and theological traditions who have encouraged me to write this book to reach a broader readership. Among these is Edward Fudge, whose biblical studies are greatly appreciated by careful students of the Bible. He has kindly consented to write the Foreword to this book and his "Seven Couplets" are found in Addendum B in this volume.

I am again indebted to the Rev. Winston Boelkins. His wise counsel and encouragement have kept me on course in writing this book as he has done before. I am most grateful to those readers of my previous book who have told me that their lives have been enriched through the thoughts I have been developing.

Neal Punt
Evergreen Park, Illinois

Note: All the texts quoted are from the Revised Standard Version except as noted.

Chapter Six appeared as an article in *Christianity Today*, March 20, 1987 and is used with permission.

To my wife and family and the members of the Evergreen Park Christian Reformed Church who provided the encouragement and atmosphere needed to produce this work with joy.

CHAPTER ONE

Two Views

YOU may have seen the silhouette of a well-proportioned vase. While looking at the vase it disappears and you see two faces against a black background. The picture seems to switch from one image to the other. The silhouette remains the same but our perception of it changes.

Our mind interprets what we see. Whether we see the faces or the vase depends on the many impressions that have been implanted in our mind throughout our lifetime. Together with these programmed influences we have the ability to concentrate our attention directing our mind to see the faces or the vase.

Something similar happens when we read the Bible. The Bible holds up before us God's wonderful plan of salvation. There are two ways of viewing the over-all message of God's Word. Which picture emerges depends on what our minds have been exposed to throughout the years.

Before we describe these views we will consider some typical

1

reactions of those who are asked to consider the two ways of picturing the message of the Bible.

Some people cannot see two pictures. One view is so deeply etched on their mind they find it impossible to see the second picture. This is understandably so among professional theologians. Suppose that for 35 years you showed visitors your heirloom - a silhouette of a vase. The impression of a vase was never questioned in your family tradition. Under such circumstances anyone claiming to see the profiles of two faces would be considered a bit odd.

Others see the two ways of viewing the Bible's message and are not impressed. It is a matter of six of one and a half dozen of the other, they say. One picture or the other does not change either the number of persons who will be saved or the way in which God saves them. Nothing actually changes so why bother about it.

Still others begin to concentrate on the new insight and it has a dramatic effect upon their life. They begin to see God, themselves, and others in a new way and it brings to them a joy, a peace, and a delight in God's plan of salvation that they had not known before.

We can see the two views by asking which of the following two statements is the over-all message of the Bible:

> A—All persons are outside of Christ (that is "lost," "condemned," "on the way to hell," "under law," "children of wrath") except those who the Bible expressly declares will be saved.

> B—All persons are elect in Christ (that is "will be saved," "justified," "on the way to heaven," "under grace," "children of God") except those who the Bible expressly declares will be finally lost.

Premise A is Commonly Used

Most Christians readily admit that they have always understood the teaching of the Bible to be that all persons are outside of Christ except those who the Bible explicitly tells us will be saved. Premise A has been deeply implanted in our mind.

It can very easily be demonstrated that *all* mainstream theology has been done on the basis of assumption A above. Those acquainted with the history of theology recognize premise A in Pelagianism, Augustinianism, Semi-Pelagianianism, Roman Catholicism, Lutheranism, Calvinism, Arminianism and in other theological traditions.

As far back as the third century theologians have worked with perspective A. Our understanding of the over-all message of the Bible has been shaped by the assumption that lies beneath every one of the traditions mentioned above.

We do not have the luxury of saying we will not adopt either A or B. In spite of all denials it is impossible to read, interpret, or proclaim the gospel without working with one view or the other. Without realizing it we necessarily work with one or the other.

It makes little difference whether we concentrate on the vase or the faces in our silhouette or if we simply smile as they endlessly switch back and forth. We may not, however, treat God's message in such a casual way. We must decide what biblical basis we have for continuing with A or B and what the practical effects of our selection will be.

The Bible speaks of two men—two "Adams." One at the dawn of history, the other "in the fullness of time." Through the disobedience of the first Adam condemnation and death came into this world. The obedience of the second Adam (Jesus Christ) brought salvation and life.

We can either so concentrate our attention on the disobedience of Adam that we see all persons involved in his condemnation and death over against a background of those who the Bible expressly tells us will come to salvation and life; or, we give Christ the place of pre-eminence and view all persons in him over against the dark shadow of those who the Bible expressly declares will be finally lost.

Premise B as Used by Charles Hodge

Dr. Charles Hodge, the Princeton Calvinist, worked with the traditional premise of seeing all persons in Adam except those who the Bible explicitly declares will be saved. On **one** occasion he caught a glimpse of the other way of viewing God's work in Christ. He then expressed our premise B (above) as follows:

> All the descendants of Adam, except Christ, are under condemnation; all the descendants of Adam, except those

of whom it is expressly revealed that they cannot inherit
the kingdom of God, are saved (*Systematic Theology*, New
York: Scribners, 1888, Vol. I, p. 26).

Within this one sentence Hodge says "All the descendants of
Adam . . . are under condemnation" and "all the descendants of
Adam . . . are saved." In **both** instances he allows **only those
exceptions** which are given in the broader context of the Bible.
Hodge found these concepts in Romans 5:18 "Then as one man's
trespass led to condemnation for all men, so one man's act of
righteousness leads to acquittal and life for all men."

When Hodge says "all the descendants of Adam . . . are saved,"
he is speaking of *objective* salvation. Objective salvation is the
work accomplished by Christ on the cross once for all, nearly 2,000
years ago. "For by a single offering he has perfected for all time
those who are sanctified" (Heb. l0:14).

In this sense all those for whom Christ died *have been* saved.
At times, therefore, the good news is declared to be "the gospel
of your salvation" [objective salvation] (Eph. 1:13). The gospel is
a declaration of what God *has done* for us and a call to respond.
It is God "who saved us and called us with a holy calling, not in
virtue of our works but in virtue of his own purpose and grace
which he gave us in Christ Jesus ages ago" (2 Tim. l:9).

The Bible also reveals a *subjective* salvation which is the
realization and application of Christ's work in the life of those for
whom Christ died. In this sense it can be said that by believing
sinners *will be* saved. The gospel "is the power of God **for**
salvation" [subjective salvation] (Rom. 1:16).

It is of utmost importance to keep in mind that premise B has
reference to *objective* salvation. In this study the expressions "elect
in Christ," "are saved" and "those who will finally be saved" will
refer to those whose salvation has been objectively accomplished
by their identity with Christ in his death and resurrection. They are
those who will surely come to fullness of new life in Christ. Their
subjective salvation, their regeneration, their new birth and conversion, may take place at any point in time during their earthly life.

A New Perspective

With the perspective provided by Hodge, all humans are to be *viewed* as elect in Christ unless we have final and decisive evidence to the contrary. With this premise we have a basis for assuming that every person we meet is a person for whom Christ died, unless we have valid reason for concluding otherwise.

If Hodge's perception is biblically valid it turns our traditional thought patterns upside down. This insight has vast implications for the way we read Scripture, are assured of our own salvation, build one another up in the faith, see the coming of Christ's kingdom, view the masses of mankind and for the approach we ought to use in evangelism.

Someone has said that words are like eyeglasses on our souls. Through words we can see our fellow workers, the people we meet on the street, and the masses of humanity, as strangers, aliens, enemies or sinners, unless we have reason to think differently about particular persons. We ought to view ourselves and all human beings as children of God, persons for whom Christ died, redeemed sinners who belong to Christ, unless we have evidence to the contrary.

It is difficult to adopt the new mind-set and do our thinking on the basis of the view presented in B (Page 2). We have been "programmed" by the instruction we received, the songs we learned and the sermons we heard, to believe that—All persons are "lost" except those who the Bible expressly declares will be saved. This assumption is so basic, so commonly held, so well accepted in every Christian tradition that it seems insolent to even question it.

It must be said, however, that this prevailing assumption has also distorted the universal accents of Scripture so that they are not accepted as an essential and joyous characteristic of the good news of the gospel. This unexamined assumption has deprived many sincere Christians of the assurance of their salvation and has often placed believers in doubt as to whether they should press the claims of Christ's kingship upon everyone everywhere. It has detracted from the positive, world-embracing, thrilling good news of what God in Christ has done for mankind. We must examine the traditional view to see whether it is biblically valid or not.

One may be inclined to say that it makes no difference whether we accept A or B (above). The actual situation will not change. The silhouette remains the same. The only thing that will change is our perception.

True reformation never begins in the world "out there." The difference will be a change within our heart and mind. Our perceptions form our attitudes. Our attitudes, in turn, affect the way we relate to God, to ourselves, and to all other human beings wherever we meet them and in whatever circumstances. Christians ought to view themselves as children of God and to view all other human beings in the same way.

Imagine for a moment that you would accept and affirm yourself and everyone you meet as an elect child of God for whom Christ died. What a reformation would take place in your life! Shouldn't we hope and pray that this perception would spread throughout the world?

Is there a biblical basis for respecting ourselves as children of God and for treating all other human beings with the same respect?

CHAPTER TWO

The Universalistic Texts

In this and the following two chapters I call attention to certain truths that may not be ignored. There are three biblical facts that must be considered in deciding whether view A or B (Page 2) reflects the teaching of God's Word.

The first fact is that there are more references in the Bible that speak of all persons coming to new life in Christ than there are those that tell us that all are condemned in Adam. It will be helpful to review some of these so-called "universalistic" passages:

> **John 1:9** The true light that enlightens every man was coming into the world.

> **John 3:17** For God sent the Son into world, not to condemn the world, but that the world might be saved through him.

> **John 12:32** And I, when I am lifted up from the earth, will draw all men to myself.

> **John 12:47** For I did not come to judge the world but to save the world.

> **Romans 5:18** Then as one man's trespass led to condemnation for all men, so one man's act of righteousness leads to acquittal and life for all men.

> **Romans 11:32** For God has consigned all men to disobedience, that he may have mercy upon all.

> **1 Corinthians 15:22** For as in Adam all die, so also in Christ shall all be made alive.

7

2 Corinthians 5:14 One has died for all: therefore all have died. And he died for all, that those who live might live no longer for themselves . . .

2 Corinthians 5:19 In Christ God was reconciling the world unto himself not counting their trespasses against them and entrusting to us the message of reconciliation.

Colossians 1:20 And through him to reconcile all things to himself, whether things on earth or in heaven, making peace by the blood of the cross.

1 Timothy 2:6 Who gave himself a ransom for all.

1 Timothy 4:10 We have our hope set on the living God, who is the Savior of all men, especially of those who believe.

Titus 2:11 For the grace of God has appeared for the salvation of all men.

Hebrews 2:9 So that by the grace of God he might taste of death for every one.

1 John 2:2 And he is the expiation for our sins, and not for ours only but also for the sins of the whole world.

Two Schools of Thought

These texts appear to teach that *everyone* will be saved. There are other passages, however, that make it abundantly clear that *not everyone* will be saved (Chapter Three). This apparent contradiction is dealt with by two schools of thought associated with the names of James Arminius and John Calvin.

Calvinists say that these texts speak of an accomplished salvation that actually saves everyone for whom Christ died. "Jesus saves," they say, "he doesn't just make salvation possible." Therefore these passages cannot be speaking of everyone in general.

Arminians are convinced that these passages refer to a salvation that God in Christ has provided for every person. "Whatever Christ has done for one sinner," they say, "he has done for every sinner." Therefore the so-called "universalistic" texts cannot have reference to a salvation which actually saves everyone for whom Christ died. They must refer to a salvation that is only a potential or possible salvation for everyone.

Calvinists cannot *demonstrate* that the "universalistic" passages do not say "all men." Arminians cannot *show* that these texts do not speak of an "actual, certain-to-be-realized" salvation. Each side discards one element or the other of the "universalistic" texts. Each side claims that to admit *both* elements would prove that everyone will be finally saved.

Throughout more than four hundred years of debate neither side has been able, by means of word studies and accepted rules of interpretation (exegesis), to demonstrate that the other side is in error in its understanding of what the "universalistic" texts assert. Both schools of thought have reason to question their over-all treatment of the "universalistic" texts.

For every ten Calvinistic scholars that are brought into the discussion to show beyond any shadow of doubt that these texts speak of "an actual, certain-to-be-realized" salvation, there are another ten Arminian theologians of equal credibility (that is— Christian, scholarly, Spirit-led, evangelical) who will just as convincingly demonstrate that these texts relate to "every person." Each side can call upon a nearly unlimited number of equally credible Lutheran and Roman Catholic reinforcement troops as needed.

One illustration of the strong evidence produced by both Arminians and Calvinists is their understanding of Romans 5:12 -21. Verse 12 reads: "Therefore as sin came into the world through one man and death through sin, and so death spread to all men because all men sinned." This text conveys at least two distinct and identifiable thoughts concerning the relationship of the "all men" to the "one man."

In the first place verse 12 tells us that sin and death *actually came* upon other persons through one man. Secondly, this text also says that the effect of sin did not come upon only *some* others, it came upon *all* other people. Arminians and Calvinists agree that **both** of these thoughts are found in verse 12.

Arminianism's "All Persons"

Arminians note that the "all men" idea is emphasized in verse 14, "even over those whose sins were not like the transgression of Adam." Verses 15 through 17 mention significant differences between the effect of Adam's deed and the work accomplished by Christ. If the work of Christ does not extend to "all" persons just as Adam's sin affected "all" persons we would expect this difference to be mentioned in verses 15 - 17.

Not only is this difference not mentioned, Paul specifically makes an application in verse 18 using the identical "all men" expression he has so clearly defined in verses 12 through 14. With *identical* words and grammatical construction he applies this same "all men" to those who are led "to acquittal and life" as well as to those who are led "to condemnation." Arminians are unmistakably correct in insisting that Romans 5:12-21 refers "acquittal and life" to all persons *just as certainly* as it declares that sin and death "spread to all men."

The appeal of Calvinists to verse 19 ("by one man's obedience *many* will be made righteous" [emphasis added]), which is used in order to limit the reference to "many" instead of "all men," is not well-taken. Verse 19 also says "by one man's disobedience *many* were made sinners." We would have to conclude that "many," not "all men" were made sinners in Adam. Whatever thought is conveyed in verse 19, it may not be used to limit the extent of the "all men" references found in verses 12 and 18.

Calvinism's "Certain-To-Be-Realized Salvation"

Calvinists, on the other hand, correctly recognize that Adam's transgression *actually brought* "sin and death" to all those represented by him (vs. 12). Paul says of those joined to Adam: "death reigned" over them, they "died," "one trespass brought condemnation," they "were made sinners" (vs. 19). By virtue of their union with Adam all men were not merely exposed to the possibility of "sin and death," they were actually "made sinners."

Of Christ's obedience Paul says it "leads to acquittal and life" just as "one man's trespass led to condemnation." If many died through one trespass "much more have the grace of God and the free gift . . . abounded for many." The free gift "brings justification." Those represented by Christ "will be made righteous." This is something quite different than saying they "will receive the opportunity to be made righteous."

Verses 15 through 17 do not say that one of the differences between Adam's transgression and Christ's obedience is that the transgression resulted in actual death while the obedience merely established a potential or possibility for life. Instead of making such a distinction, Paul, using the *identical* grammatical construction, makes a parallel application of actual death and actual life in verse 18. Calvinists are unmistakably correct in noting that Romans 5:12 through 21 says "acquittal and life" actually come to all those represented by Christ *just as certainly* as it declares that "sin and death" actually came upon all those represented by Adam.

Both Are Right

Arminians and Calvinists together have produced convincing evidence that Romans 5:12 through 21 speaks of actual, certain-to-be-realized salvation and it does so in relationship to all persons. Both schools of thought have produced similar irrefutable evidence for the positive declarations they find in the other so-called "universalistic" passages. (See Neal Punt, *Unconditional Good News*, Wm. B. Eerdmans Publishing Co., 1980, pp. 9-16, 31-55.)

The "universalistic" texts read in Greek just as they do in our accepted English translations. They speak of "actual, certain-to-be-realized" salvation as Calvinists have consistently maintained, and they do so in relationship to "all persons" as the Arminians have always affirmed.

Calvinists, using every legitimate means available to them, have failed to demonstrate that Arminians are in error in insisting that the "universalistic" texts speak of all persons. This four centuries of failure is owing to the fact that Arminians are not wrong in holding firmly to the view that these passages speak of all persons.

Arminians have been just as unsuccessful in more than 400 years of diligent effort to show that Calvinists are mistaken in their view that the "universalistic" texts speak of an accomplished, certain-to-be-realized salvation. No progress toward a common understanding of the basic teachings of God's Word has been made and none **can be made** until both sides acknowledge that the so-called "universalistic" texts speak of accomplished, certain-to-be-realized salvation and they do so in reference to all people.

Anyone reading these passages (in English or Greek) within their immediate context can come to no other conclusion than that they speak of all persons coming to new life in Christ. This is not a matter of textual criticism, interpretation, or any sleight of hand. These passages plainly speak of a certain-to-be-realized (not merely a potential) salvation and they do so in terms of all persons.

What Happens Now?

We may not like it. It may not fit into the way we have structured our theology. It may change the way we view questions concerning who will be saved and who will be finally lost as well as how they are saved and the basis upon which some will be finally lost. But what may not be ignored and cannot be refuted is the fact that—**the "universalistic" texts speak of a certain-to-be-realized salvation in terms of all persons.**

I make the above claim in my book *Unconditional Good News.* The response has been amazing. Many knowledgeable Arminians and Calvinists (pastors, denominational leaders, professors, authors and others) seemed to breathe a collective sigh of relief and say in effect: "Neither have we been comfortable with the way our theological tradition has dealt with the 'universalistic' passages."

Both Calvinists and Arminians are reluctant to make such an admission until they are assured that the other side is willing to admit that they also may have taken a wrong turn. Both sides are very much concerned that to accept the "universalistic" passages just as we find them in our English (and Greek) Bible seems to play into the hands of those who teach that all persons will come to salvation in Christ. We shall address this legitimate concern in Chapter Five (below).

To determine whether premise A or B (Page 2) reflects the over-all teaching of the Bible we must reckon with this our first fact, this **biblical given: the "universalistic" texts, within their immediate context, speak of an accomplished, certain-to-be-realized salvation and they do so in relationship to all persons in general.** In other words, we must accept these passages just as we find them in our English (and Greek) Bible.

CHAPTER THREE

Some Will Be Lost

FEW truths are more obvious to most Christians than that the Bible teaches that there will be a final division of mankind. Some will be saved and some will be finally lost. It hardly seems necessary to call the reader's attention to the fact that some will be finally lost.

Views concerning the nature and purpose of the final judgment (hell) range from annihilationism (cease to exist) to retribution (suffering in body and soul throughout eternity). Although important, the nature of eternal death is not the concern of this chapter. Whatever its nature the biblical truth is that some persons will be subject to eternal death.

Absolute Universalism

Ever since the third century there have been those who claim that all the descendants of Adam will be saved. God's judgment against sin is temporary, they say. Its purpose is to purge us from sin, teach us to hate evil and to recognize Christ as our Savior.

The teaching that all will find salvation in Christ, either in this life or in a future existence is called Universalism or Absolute Universalism (or Restoration Theology). This view is commonly found in liberal theology and, strange as it may seem, it is finding an increasing acceptance among evangelical Christians today. "It is a consummation devoutly to be wished," as Shakespeare might say. But wishing does not make it so.

Universalism is among the most appealing and destructive errors seeping into the church today. It is in essence the original

13

lie of Satan "You will not die." It is more deceptive than in its original form because it comes cloaked as the perfect work accomplished by Christ. This lie has a sympathetic appeal for all who are asking (and many are asking), "What about those millions of pagans who live and die without ever hearing about the way of salvation in Jesus Christ?" We take up this question in Chapter Thirteen.

Absolute Universalists use the very best work done by Arminians to show that the so-called "universalistic" passages do refer to "all persons." They take a similar invaluable harvest from the hundreds of years of careful study by Calvinists, demonstrating that these texts are talking about a certain-to-be-realized salvation, and not merely a potential or possible salvation. The facts as we disclosed them in the previous chapter do work to the advantage of Universalists.

However, our concern to refute the error of Universalism does not give us license to distort or deny what those passages clearly say. Furthermore, if we deny that the so-called "universalistic" texts speak of a certain-to-be-realized salvation in relationship to all persons, we thereby surrender to the Absolute Universalists the strongest grammatical evidence for their *exclusive* use. Knowledgeable students of Scripture are beginning to recognize the futility of such denial.

To effectively refute the teaching of Universalism one must accept the so-called "universalistic" texts just as we find them in our English (and Greek) Bible. We must then demonstrate that accepting the obvious, clear, overt declarations of these passages does not lead to the teaching that all persons will be saved. We shall proceed to that important task in Chapter Five.

Universal salvation is a false hope and it is shown to be false by the repeated biblical accounts of a final separation. All the arguments put forth by Universalists cannot be addressed in this brief chapter. Our limited purpose is to call attention to two subtle arguments that are frequently used by Universalists. Both of these arguments have strong appeal because they are based on assumptions which many evangelical Christians accept without having examined the validity of those assumptions.

Not All Are Children of God

The first argument is that human parents never abandon their children except for the fact that parents are sinful or weak. From this one can conclude that God, the ideal Father, with his unlimited ability and resources will never finally forsake any member of his own family. To suggest that God would abandon his own children is an insult to God. Even if a woman can "forget her sucking child" (Isa. 49:15), God will not forget his children. It *necessarily* follows "If children, then heirs" (Rom. 8:17).

If the assumption upon which this argument is built is valid, the argument is irrefutable. The assumption is that all persons are children of God by virtue of their creation in the image of God. This assumption is seldom challenged by evangelical Christians.

Although the Bible reveals that Adam and Eve were created in the image of God, it does not tell us they were created as children of God. Even sinless human beings would have to be adopted into God's family. The one reference which appears to say that Adam was the son of God by creation ("Adam, the son of God" [Luke 3:38]) means no more than that Adam "came from" God. The words "the son of" are not found in the Greek and for some of those listed in this genealogy there are many generations between the two persons mentioned even though the translation reads "the son of."

Furthermore, when the Bible says that all persons are "made from one [blood]" and that we are "God's offspring" it does so in order to draw certain conclusions concerning the kind of God who made us. "What therefore you worship as unknown, this I proclaim to you" (see Acts 17:23-29). The Bible *never* uses these facts to draw the conclusion that all persons are children of God, and neither may we do so.

The modern phrasing for Satan's seductive assurance "You will not die" (Gen. 3:4) is: "We are the human family together for the Father made us all," or "We have one Father, even God." These deductions from our common creation contradict the clear words of Jesus "You are of your father the devil," "You are not of God" (John 8:41, 44, 47).

Biological ancestry does not make all human beings members of God's family. "Do not presume to say to yourselves, 'We have Abraham as our father'; for I tell you, God is able from these stones to raise up children to Abraham" (Matt. 3:9). The stuff we are made of, whether a common ancestry or stones, does not make us one human family together with either Abraham or God as our father.

Scripture knows of only two ways to be part of God's family: through natural generation ("Christ alone is the eternal, natural son of God") and by adoption ("we are adopted children of God"). To look to creation as a basis for viewing all persons as belonging to one family is to confuse the creational and redemptive work of God. Creational unity, such as it was, has been broken by sin and is restored only in Christ. Redemptive unity is not shared by all persons. The human brotherhood ("the human family together") of which the Bible speaks extends as far as those who "do the will of my [Jesus'] Father" and no farther (Matt. 12: 49, 50).

None Are of Infinite Value

A second argument made by Absolute Universalists is that every person will be saved because each one created in God's image is of infinite value. Again, the argument cannot be refuted if the basic assumption is granted. God is neither so foolish nor so weak as to be deprived of something that has infinite value.

This argument appeals to the fact that Christians appreciate the extremely high value of every human being. We accept the hyperbole "the human person created in the image of God has infinite value." So much practical good would evolve if every human being were treated as though he or she had infinite value, that we would like to think that this hyperbole is literally true. But the fact is that nothing created can be of infinite value. If it were, the essential distinction between the Creator and that which is created would be breached.

To say God will save every sinner because every human being has infinite value does serious injustice to the gracious character of God's saving act. It would follow that God saves for value to be received. God's motivation in saving sinners would be that of a man who has found a "hidden treasure" or a "pearl of great price" (Matt. 13:44, 45). This contradicts the theme found throughout all of Scripture that he saved us "in virtue of his own purpose and grace (undeserved favor) which he gave us in Christ Jesus" (2 Tim. I:9). The high price God paid on the cross for our salvation was owing to God's holiness, not man's created worth. Out of loyalty not only to the express declarations of Scripture but also in the light of the graciousness of God's saving act, we *must* recognize that human beings are not of infinite value.

A Final Separation

Universalists insist that we must accept the clear, overt declarations of the so-called "universalistic" texts just as we find them in our English (and Greek) Bible. Rightly so. We must also accept the obvious meaning of the many passages of Scripture which expressly declare that there will be a final division among the children of men. (For one of the most competent and thorough studies of both Old and New Testament evidence for the doctrine of final separation, see Edward Fudge, *The Fire That Consumes*, Providential Press, P. O. Box 218026, Houston, TX, 77218.)

Some persons will be separated from the eternal, joyous, presence of God. Among the express declarations of Scripture are these:

> **Matthew 7:23** Then will I declare to them, "I never knew you; depart from me, you evil doers."

> **Matthew 25:41** Then he will say to those at his left hand, "Depart from me, you cursed, into the eternal fire prepared for the devil and his angels."

> **Matthew 25:46** And they will go away into eternal punishment, but the righteous into eternal life.

> **John 5:28, 29** For the hour is coming when all who are in the tombs will hear his voice and come forth, those who have done good, to the resurrection of life, and those who have done evil, to the resurrection of judgment.

> **2 Thessalonians 1:9** They shall suffer the punishment of eternal destruction and exclusion from the presence of the Lord and from the glory of his might, when he comes.

> **2 Thessalonians 2:12** So that all may be condemned who did not believe the truth but had pleasure in unrighteousness.

Revelation 22:15 Outside are the dogs and sorcer-
ers and fornicators and murderers and idolaters,
and everyone who loves and practices falsehood.

Those evangelicals who believe that they find Absolute Universalism taught in the Bible should learn from the history of the
Unitarians (those who deny that God exists in three persons, Father,
Son and Holy Spirit). They firmly held to an infallible Bible and
to their Unitarian views. When it became evident that they could
not hold to both, they chose to compromise their view of the
Scriptures. Sooner or later those who hold to universal salvation
will have to choose between their cherished belief that all persons
will be saved and their acceptance of an infallible Bible.

In the preceding chapter we saw that the so-called "universalistic" texts speak of an accomplished, certain-to-be-realized salvation, and they do so in reference to all persons. This is so massively
and clearly evident that it must be accepted as a biblical given.
The **second biblical fact** that must be taken into account in deciding
between premise A and B (Page 2), is that the Bible teaches
that—**some persons will be finally lost.**

CHAPTER FOUR

Those Who Will Be Lost

WHEN Hodge says "all the descendants of Adam . . . are saved" (Page 3 - 4) he acknowledges that there are exceptions. Hodge describes those who will not be saved as "those of whom it is expressly revealed that they cannot enter the kingdom of God."

We must determine from the express declarations of Scripture who will experience God's final judgment. Notice carefully the question is **not** "Who deserves eternal death?"

Due to the Fall and disobedience of our first parents Adam and Eve in Paradise, all persons, except Jesus Christ, are conceived and born in sin. Consequently everyone deserves eternal death. Universal human corruption and blameworthiness is taught throughout Scripture. This is the doctrine of original sin.

Romans 1:18 - 3:20 and parallel passages speak of the reality of human existence apart from the regenerating and renewing work of the Holy Spirit. They are a description of every person who is not born again and a picture of every child of God before he or she was born again. They reveal the fact that "All have turned aside, together they have gone wrong; no one does good, not even one" (Rom. 3:12).

Not All Are Outside of Christ

At this point we must take note of a significant error made in every theological tradition. They have taken the scriptural doctrine of original sin as evidence that all persons, as a result of their sin in Adam, are **outside of Christ.** This error accounts in large measure for the fact that traditionally we feel very comfortable with premise A (Page 2)—All persons *are outside of Christ* except those who the Bible expressly declares will be saved.

The doctrine of original sin does not tell us that all persons are *outside of Christ*. The fact that **all persons are sinners in Adam** is neither synonymous nor coterminous (having the same boundary or limits) with the idea that **all persons are outside of Christ.** These concepts **may not** be interchanged.

It is one thing to say that all persons are by nature children of wrath and worthy of eternal death. It is something **altogether different** to say that all persons are outside of Christ. The doctrine of original sin does not tell us whether many or few, all or none, of those involved in it will be finally lost. The teaching of original sin does not distinguish those who will be saved from those who will be finally lost.

The fact that all the descendants of Adam (except Jesus Christ) are joined with Adam in his sin and its consequences tells us **nothing** about who is or is not joined with Christ in his death and resurrection. Romans 1:18 - 3:20 and parallel passages cannot be the starting point, the foundation stone, (the *prolegomenon*), for developing a doctrine of salvation by claiming that those who will be saved are exceptions to those described in these passages.

There is no basis for claiming that those who will be saved are exceptions to those described in Romans 1:18-3:20. From the fact that all persons (except Jesus Christ) are sinful by nature we may not conclude that all persons are outside of Christ.

Premise B (Page 2) accepts the biblical doctrine of original sin. Due to the sin of Adam all persons, except Jesus Christ, are not only worthy of eternal judgment but they will actually suffer eternal death on the basis of their sin in Adam *unless* the sovereign electing grace of God intervenes to rescue them from such a fate.

What has been overlooked, however, by every school of theology is that the good news is that the electing grace of God *does intervene* on behalf of every person except those who, throughout all their life, willfully and finally "refuse to have God in their knowledge."

To develop a biblical doctrine of **sin** we must begin with Adam and note who is represented by and joined to him in the Fall. The Bible tells us that all persons, with one exception, were made sinners through the one sin of Adam.

To understand the Bible's teaching concerning **salvation** we must begin with Jesus Christ and learn who is represented by and united with him in his work of redemption. The Bible tells us that all persons, with certain exceptions, will be made righteous in Christ.

That this is the biblical pattern for structuring the doctrine of salvation is demonstrated by the fact that the following texts move directly, within the confines of a single text, from the perspective of seeing all persons in the First Adam to viewing all persons in the Second Adam.

> **Romans 5:18** Then as one man's trespass led to condemnation for all men, so one man's act of righteousness leads to acquittal and life for all men.

> **Romans 11:32** For God has consigned all men to disobedience, that he may have mercy upon all.

> **1 Corinthians 15:22** For as in Adam all die, so also in Christ shall all be made alive.

We must accept these and all the other so-called "universalistic" texts just as we find them in our English (and Greek) Bible, allowing only for the exceptions the Bible itself makes (Chapter Five, below).

Some Are Outside of Christ

How does the Bible describe the exceptions, those who are "outside of Christ," those who "cannot enter the kingdom of God," those who will be finally lost, "the reprobate"?

In 1977 the Christian Reformed Church received a formal complaint against its creedal teaching on reprobation. "The essence, the heart, the soul" of the complaint was that one of its creeds (the *Canons of Dort*) teaches that some persons are "consigned to everlasting damnation before they ever came into being." The complaint never questioned the fact that all the descendants of Adam, except Jesus Christ, are **worthy of** everlasting damnation.

To emphatically deny "the essence, the heart" of this complaint a three year study was adopted and referred "to the churches for elucidation of the teaching of the *Canons* on election and reprobation." This **official** "elucidation" states:

"God consigns someone to destruction [hell] only on the basis of what that person does; and whatever evil actions that person performs." "God condemns to destruction [hell] only those who do, in fact, exhibit unbelief." All non-elect persons are "the agents of unbelief" [An agent is one who himself acts.]. "The condition of the non-elect [headed for hell] results from their unbelief." "The basis for that condemnation [being sent to hell] is to be found solely in the persistent unbelief and sin of those so condemned." (See *1980 Acts of Synod*, Christian Reformed Publications, p. 593.)

These references speak of **all those** who are consigned to hell. They declare that such consignment *never* occurs **apart from** individual, willful, final (persistent), unbelief and sin on the part of the person so condemned.

The critical question was this: Do the *Canons of Dort* teach or *allow for the possibility* that some persons are "consigned to everlasting damnation" **solely** on the basis of their sin in Adam? To answer **yes** to this question would concede "the essence, the heart" of the complaint, namely, some persons are "consigned to everlasting damnation before they ever came into being." Therefore a most emphatic **no** was given, as the above quotations clearly show.

This official "elucidation" is not consistent with what has been the historic position of the Reformed churches regarding the doctrine of reprobation. This "elucidation" removes an ambiguity that may have been purposely left in the *Canons of Dort* because the authors were not of one mind concerning this critical question.

A Willful Choice

What is important for our present concern is that this three year study removes the ambiguity and thereby accurately reflects the teaching of Scripture regarding all those who will be finally lost—the reprobate.

On the one hand, throughout the Bible we consistently find that all persons, due to the sin of Adam, are sinners by nature and are *worthy of* eternal death. On the other hand, nowhere in all of Scripture do we read—nor is it implied, nor is it to be inferred—that anyone ever suffers eternal death by reason of their sin in Adam, **apart from** individual, willful, final unbelief and sin on the part of the person so rejected. (See Punt, *Unconditional Good News*, pp. 24-26.)

Neither premise B (Page 2) nor the above mentioned "elucidation" denies that original sin is the basis for condemnation. Both premise B and this **official** "elucidation" deny that original sin is ever the basis for consignment to everlasting damnation **apart from** personal, individual, willful, persistent sin on the part of the person so condemned.

Therefore this biblical insight does not lead to the conclusion that no one will suffer the consequences of their sin in Adam or that the guilt of Adam's sin has been removed for all persons. The only warranted conclusion is that God has chosen not to carry out the sentence of eternal judgment except on those individuals who, in addition to their sin in Adam, finally persist in following their own ways, making their own personal decisions against God.

We must not think that *only those* who hear the gospel can make "their own personal decisions against God." "Ever since the creation of the world his invisible nature, namely, his eternal power and deity, has been clearly perceived in the things that have been made. So they are without excuse; for although they knew God they did not honor him as God or give thanks to him, but they became futile in their thinking and their senseless minds were darkened" (Rom. 1:20, 21).

Furthermore, "They show that what the law requires is written on their hearts, while their conscience also bears witness and their conflicting thoughts accuse or perhaps excuse them" (Rom. 2:15). To reject or remain indifferent to God's revelation of himself in creation and in "their conscience" is sufficient to convict people of sin and to leave them without excuse whether they hear the gospel or not.

Disregard of God's will can be expressed not only in doing what is contrary to it; it can also be evidenced in doing nothing. Those who stand before the will of God for their lives (whether expressed in creation/conscience or gospel proclamation) and choose to ignore what is made known to them are not without guilt for their indifference. "Whoever knows what is right to do and fails to do it, for him it is sin" (James 4:17).

Those Who Will Be Finally Lost

The Bible tells us that there are two categories or classifications of persons who will be eternally separated from the presence of God. "All who have sinned without the law will also perish without the law, and all who have sinned under the law will be judged by the law" (Rom. 2:12). There are those who will be "without excuse" because they did not honor God as he made made himself known "in the things that have been made" (Rom. 1:19-21); and those who "are condemned" because they have "not believed in the name of the only Son of God" (John 3:18).

The analogy has been made: There are moths that persistently attack the candle's flame until the flame consumes them. There are other moths that grow indifferent to the glow of the candle and drift away into the darkness. So it is with all those who will not experience the light and joy of living eternally in God's presence. Some attack God's majesty until they are consumed by it. Others by their indifference separate themselves from God's abiding presence. In either case final separation never takes place **apart from** the individual, willful, final (persistent) unbelief and sin of the particular person who is eternally separated from God's joyous presence.

This is our **third biblical given** that must be taken into consideration when making our decision between A and B (Page 2). **Those who will be finally lost are those, and only those, who, in addition to their sin in Adam, throughout their entire life, willfully and finally reject or remain indifferent toward whatever revelation of himself God has given to them.**

CHAPTER FIVE

Generalizations

WE began this study by saying that we must decide which of the following two views reflects the teaching of Scripture:

> A - All persons are outside of Christ (that is "lost," "condemned," "on the way to hell," "under law," "children of wrath") except those who the Bible expressly declares will be saved.

> B - All persons are elect in Christ (that is "will be saved," "justified," "on the way to heaven," "under grace," "children of God") except those who the Bible expressly declares will be finally lost.

The first fact that must be considered in order to decide between A and B is that the so-called "universalistic" texts speak of an actual, certain-to-be-realized salvation and that they do so in reference to all persons. Because the church has traditionally worked on the basis of assumption A, it has been forced either to deny the universal element ("all persons") or to reject the realized salvation aspect ("are saved") of the so-called "universalistic" texts (Chapter Two).

Human Nature Has Faces

If we accept **both** the "certain-to-be-realized" **and** the "all persons" aspects of the "universalistic" texts, must we not conclude that all persons will be saved? To avoid this conclusion the suggestion has been made that these texts refer to "race-salvation." That is to say,

25

even though some individual members are not saved, the organic unit called the "human race," "humanity," or "human nature" is finally saved in God's redemption plan.

The difficulty with this solution is that "human race," "humanity" and so on, are concepts that exist only in the realm of thought. As important as such abstract concepts are, and although it can be said that the human race will exist in heaven (also in hell, for that matter), it cannot be said that **the human race** was the object of Christ's atonement.

Suppose a severe famine threatens the extinction of the human race in a particular place. One cannot feed or provide for the needs of "the human race" which is common to the people of that area without actually feeding and providing for a definite number of those people, either all of them or some of them.

So also Jesus came to save people—"by one man's obedience *many* will be made righteous" (Rom. 5:19, emphasis added). Forgiveness of sins and resurrection life cannot be given to *the human race* without granting forgiveness and bringing salvation to a definite number of persons, either all of them or some of them.

Generalizations, Not Universal Statements

Rather than trying to find the solution in an abstract "race salvation," we can accept **both** the "all persons" **and** the "realized salvation" elements of the "universalistic" texts if we recognize the difference between generalizations and universal statements. There is a world of difference between universal statements and generalizations, although we often confuse the two.

Universals by definition allow no exceptions. Generalizations are universal declarations that have known exceptions. Every theological tradition has failed to recognize that the so-called "universalistic" texts are generalizations, **not** universals. This has caused significant divisions within the Christian church.

Because they insist that these texts are universals, Calvinists conclude that such passages must make reference to all persons in Christ *without exception*. Barth claims they must teach that all persons are elect in Christ *without exception*. Arminians say that they must speak of a potential salvation for all persons *without exception*. Absolute Univeralists say that they must proclaim actual salvation for all persons *without exception*.

It is essential to realize that whenever the Bible speaks of the fact that in Adam "All die" or in Christ "All should be made alive," it *invariably* allows for exceptions. Not one of the so-called "universalistic" texts is a universal. Every one of them is a generalization.

The following confessional statement expresses the meaning of Romans 5:18a ("One man's trespass led to condemnation for all men"): "The corruption spread, by God's just judgment, from Adam to *all* his descendants—*except for Christ alone . . .* by way of the propagation of his [Adam's] perverted nature" (*Canons of Dort*, III-IV, 2, emphasis added).

Neither Romans 5:18a nor Romans 5:12 "Death spread to all men because all men sinned" are universals. They are generalizations because they have an exception, namely, the one who is the "seed of the woman," "the son of man," the one "born of the virgin Mary."

Even though Romans 5:18a says "One man's trespass led to condemnation for all men," there was not "condemnation for all men." Jesus did not share in the Fall when the descendants of Adam were "made sinners by" Adam's disobedience (Rom. 5:19). Jesus was not "conceived and born in sin." Now, in spite of this exception, the over-all message of Scripture is "In Adam's fall, we sinned all."

Neither Romans 5:18b "One man's act of righteousness leads to acquittal and life for all men," nor the other so-called "universalistic" texts are universals. Every one of them is a generalization. "They shall suffer the punishment of eternal destruction and exclusion from the presence of the Lord" (2 Thess. 1:9) and other passages (see Page 17) make it abundantly clear that there are exceptions. In spite of the exceptions, the over-all message of Scripture is "All men come to justification of life."

Generalizations in the Bible

Whatever the Bible says it says from within its entire context. When the "universalistic" texts speak of accomplished, actual, certain-to-be-realized salvation in terms of all persons, they may **never** be understood apart from the exceptions that are found in the broader context of Scripture. These texts are like fish out of water, having no sustainable life of their own when they are read in isolation from the rest of the Bible.

The Bible alerts us to the fact that its universal declarations may have exceptions that are not found in the immediate context. "For God has put all things in subjection under his feet" (1 Cor. 15:27). This universal declaration taken from Psalm 8:6 is also found in Hebrews 2:8 with a qualifying phrase added, underscoring its universal thrust: "Now in putting everything in subjection to him, he left nothing outside his control."

This clear-cut, emphatic *universal declaration* has an exception. First Corinthians 15:27 continues: "But when it [the Bible] says, 'All things are put in subjection under him,' it is plain that he is excepted who put all things under him."

We can use a parallel of 1 Corinthians 15:27 to express the view we are contending for in this study: "The Bible says [in the "universalistic" texts] that all persons are elect in Christ. But when it says 'All persons are elect in Christ,' it is plain that those are excepted of whom the Bible says they will not inherit the kingdom of God."

In the light of what we find in 1 Corinthians 15:27 one may well wonder if the Bible **ever** makes a universal declaration that **does not** have exceptions. Notice—"All things are lawful for me," says Paul (1 Cor. 6:12); there were exceptions. "With God all things are possible" Matt. 19:26; yet God "cannot deny himself" (2 Tim. 2:13). Prayers should be made "for all men" (1 Timothy 2:1); but not for the dead and possibly not for some others (1 John 5:16). "All who are in Asia turned away from me" (2 Tim. 1:15); and the following verse speaks of an exception, and so on.

Practically every universal declaration in Scripture has known exceptions and is therefore a generalization. Each of these generalizations expresses a general truth. God *did* put all things under Christ's feet. All things *were* lawful for Paul. With God all things *are* possible. We *are* exhorted to pray for all persons. All *did* turn away from Paul. The exceptions do not negate the basic truth set forth in the generalization.

We make a serious error either if we do not accept the truth proclaimed by these generalizations, or if we overlook the exceptions which must be understood from the broader context of Scripture.

The Purpose of Generalizations

What purpose do generalizations serve? They can be very confusing because they appear to break the law of noncontradiction. Murder, adultery and blasphemy were **not** "lawful for" Paul. Nevertheless, Paul says "All things are lawful for me" (1 Cor. 6:12). How can Scripture say both "All things *are* lawful for" Paul and **"Not** all things *are* lawful for" Paul? How can there be such a straight and flat contradiction in Scripture? Isn't the law of noncontradiction valid?

Generalizations do not violate the law of noncontradiction. Generalizations reveal the mind-set with which the author is working. They give expression to the perspective from which the matter at hand is to be viewed.

In 1 Corinthians 6:12 Paul celebrates the new mind-set of Christian liberty. Instead of being a legalist, as many around him still were, viewing all things as unlawful except what the law permitted, Paul has a glorious new view, a new perspective, a new freedom in Christ. He has come to realize that "all things **are** lawful" for him! It being understood, of course, that those things and only those things specifically forbidden by God were not lawful for him.

So also the so-called "universalistic" texts reveal the mind-boggling change that has taken place through the work of Christ. We no longer see all persons in Adam, outside of Christ, on the way to hell, with some specifically mentioned exceptions. We now see "the world," "all persons," "everyone" as elect in Christ, certain-to-come-to-salvation, except for those specifically mentioned exceptions who will be finally lost.

Generalizations Make a Difference

It is exceedingly difficult to recognize that our reading of Scripture, as well as our theologizing, is colored by our mind-set (the generalization with which we work). It is even more difficult to change that mind-set. Most of the time we are not aware of the assumption with which we work. Our mind-set will determine **what we see** in Scripture.

Reacting negatively to the premise I am seeking to establish, a well-known theologian wrote to me: "Salvation is a gift conditional upon response. As in Hebrews 4:2, real good news but not of benefit until mixed with faith." Turning to Hebrews 4:2 we find that it says, "For good news came to us just as to them; but the message which they heard did not benefit them, because it did not meet with faith in the hearers."

Those who approach Hebrews 4:2 with the assumption "All are outside of Christ except . . ." (Premise A) will understand this verse to say —the good news comes indiscriminately to all persons, and those who benefit from it do so *because* they believe. That is how my objector understood the verse.

However, those who approach Hebrews 4:2 with the assumption "All are elect in Christ, except . . ." (Premise B) will understand this verse to teach—the good news is proclaimed indiscriminately to all persons and all persons are its beneficiaries, except those who refuse to believe.

Hebrews 4:2 does not tell us which assumption is correct. Nevertheless, the assumption we work with will affect our understanding of this verse. Consider—Does Hebrews 4:2 say some benefited *because they believed*? Or does it say, some did not benefit *because they did not believe*? (Undecided? See vs. 6.) If it is the later, isn't this a bit more consistent with premise B?

Arminians and Calvinists have worked with assumption A—All persons are outside of Christ except those who the Bible specifically declares will be saved. It is this mind-set that got them at loggerheads in the first place.

If **both** traditions would switch to mind-set B—All persons are elect in Christ except those who the Bible specifically declares will be finally lost, they could accept the clear, overt, reading of the so-called "universalistic" texts just as we find them in our English (and Greek) Bible. With premise B there is the possibility of positive, fruitful, discussions between Arminians and Calvinists.

How do we arrive at premise B instead of A? We do so by means of these three facts, **three biblical givens:**

> **Fact # 1,**—The so-called "universalistic" texts, within their immediate context, speak of a certain-to-be-realized salvation and they do so in relationship to all persons in general (Chapter Two).

> **Fact # 2,**—Not all persons will come to new life in Christ, some will be finally lost (Chapter Three).

Fact # 3,—Those who will be finally lost are only those, who, in addition to their sin in Adam, willfully, personally, and finally reject whatever revelation God has given of himself to them (Chapter Four).

We may not change these biblical givens to make them conform to our unexamined assumption. Our assumption must be made to conform to these biblically revealed facts.

We can account for these three facts **only** by allowing them to establish, to mold, to frame, to form our perspective, our mind-set, so that we understand the message of Scripture to be—All persons are elect in Christ except those who the Bible expressly declares will be finally lost.

CHAPTER SIX

Biblical Universalism

THE silhouette of the vase and the faces (Chapter One) reminds us that we tend to see what we want or have been trained to see. We noted that something similar happens when we read the Bible. Scripture reading is based on an assumption and we tend to validate our assumption in the way we read Scripture.

Our understanding of the over-all message of the Bible depends on which of the following two assumptions we work with:

A - All persons are outside of Christ except those who the Bible expressly declares will be saved.

B - All persons are elect in Christ except those who the Bible expressly declares will be finally lost.

A Long History

Although Hodge used presupposition B in the reference cited (Page 3 - 4), there is no evidence that he ever used this premise in the rest of his writings. Even more perplexing is the fact that in the history of the interpretation of the "all" and "every" texts, one does not find B either suggested or refuted. The nearly unanimous acceptance of premise A throughout the centuries can probably be accounted for by the following considerations:

1) All persons, except Jesus Christ, are children of wrath by nature, inclined to do evil and deserving of eternal death. From the biblical doctrine of original sin the conclusion was erroneously

drawn that all persons are outside of Christ except those who the Bible expressly declares will be saved. Romans 1:18-3:20 and parallel passages became, and continue to be, the wrong starting point (*prolegomenon*) for structuring the doctrine of salvation (Chapter Four).

2) Viewing all persons as "lost" in Adam with some exceptions (those who would be saved) continued to be the basis for developing theology throughout the centuries. The history of theology can be traced in terms of how the various theological traditions perceived of the way in which these exceptions come to salvation out of a "lost" humanity (Chapter Ten, below).

This perspective continued because the only challenge to it came from the Absolute Universalists (those who teach that all persons will be saved). The church instinctively knew that such was not the over-all message of Scripture and summarily rejected that teaching (rightly so).

The third century teaching that all the descendants of Adam will be saved became the first doctrine to be declared heretical by a world-wide assembly of the church. Since that time, the suggestion that there is a sense in which it can be said that the righteousness of Christ "leads to justification and life for all men" (Rom. 5:18b) became *unthinkable* for all main-stream theology.

A Biblical Pattern

This concern to refute Universalism is legitimate. Absolute Universalism cannot be an option for those who acknowledge the authority of the Scriptures. However, over-reaction to this teaching so that we close our eyes to certain biblically revealed facts hinders our ability to understand the good news.

Among the biblical givens that must be accounted for are the following **three facts:** 1) the "universalistic" texts speak of accomplished salvation in relationship to all persons (Chapter Two); 2) some persons will be lost (Chapter Three); and, 3) those who will be lost are those and only those who in addition to their sin in Adam throughout their lifetime refuse to have God in their knowledge (Chapter Four).

These biblical givens can be held in a tension-filled unity by recognizing that the so-called "universalistic" texts are not universals, they are generalizations (Chapter Five). That is, they are universal statements which have known exceptions. Generalizations are a common way of expressing the writer's perspective (mind-set), from which the matter at hand is to be viewed.

Premise B accounts for the above facts. This premise is also consistent with the way God has dealt with mankind throughout history. He created man good and in a right relationship to himself. "And God blessed them" (Gen. 1:28). This blessedness of knowing God and living in fellowship with him was not something conferred upon mankind in response to or merited by obedience. However, these blessings and fellowship with God would no longer be enjoyed if man refused to live in obedience to God's revealed will. "You may freely eat of every tree of the garden; but of the tree of the knowledge of good and evil you shall not eat, for in the day you eat of it you shall die" (Gen. 2:16b, 17).

Mankind's relationship to God followed this pattern: "You were blameless in your ways from the day you were created, till iniquity was found in you" (Ezek. 28:14). The blessing was unconditional, the judgment had to be earned.

Again, when establishing his covenant with Abraham, God did not propose or prescribe certain conditions so that by keeping them Abraham could attain a favorable status with God. "And I will make of you a great nation, and I will bless you, and make your name great so that you will be a blessing" (Gen. 12:2). "And I will establish my covenant between me and you and your descendants after you throughout their generations for an everlasting covenant, to be God to you and your descendants after you" (Gen. 17:7), was God's promised goodness to Abraham and his descendants before those descendants were born.

Abraham and his descendants would enjoy the unearned blessing and favor of God unless and until they refused to believe in him or to live in obedience to him. The blessing was unconditional, the judgment was contingent upon man's action.

God affirmed his covenant with the entire nation of Israel at Mt. Sinai. He made his will known to them and gave them the Ten Commandments. The commandments were not given so that by keeping them the Israelites could become the recipients of God's favor. They already were God's adopted children. "When Israel was a child, I loved him, and out of Egypt I called my son" (Hos. 11:1). The commandments came to Israel with the assurance "I am the Lord your God who brought you out of the land of Egypt, out of the house of bondage" (Exod. 20:2).

They were the recipients of God's blessing. It was also true that if they willfully and finally refused to walk in accordance with God's revealed will, they would not experience his blessing or live in fellowship with him.

God's favor and blessing at the time of creation, in the call of Abraham and in the affirmation of covenantal blessings at Mt. Sinai were not given on the basis of faith, obedience, holiness or any other good quality or disposition in man as a prerequisite, cause or condition for those blessings. In the light of this history we have reason to expect that salvation would also come as an announcement of unconditional good news accompanied with a threat of judgment conditional upon disobedience. Salvation is by grace, condemnation is by works.

The good news is that the obedience of the Second Adam has overcome all the dreadful effects of the disobedience of the First Adam except for those persons who, throughout all their life, willfully and finally refuse to have God in their knowledge. That is to say—All persons are elect in Christ except those who the Scripture expressly declares will be finally lost.

A Few Clarifications

It may be helpful to think of premise B as a *qualified* Universalism. The necessary limiting qualification to Universalism is so clearly revealed in Scripture that I do not hesitate to call this premise Biblical Universalism.

This new perspective or view of the over-all message of Scripture is so foreign to our traditional way of thinking that it raises many questions. The following observations will help us understand the perspective of Biblical Universalism:

1) Biblical Universalism does not say that we should assume that all persons are converted, are born again or that they are Christians. We are to assume they are *elect in Christ* unless we have decisive and final evidence to the contrary. Their subjective salvation, their regeneration, their new birth and conversion may take place at any point in time during their earthly life.

2) We must also carefully notice that in saying "All the descendants of Adam . . . are saved" (Page 3 - 4) and allowing only for

biblically declared exceptions, Hodge does not say or imply that all persons are initially elect in Christ but that subsequently some of them are removed from this union with Christ.

Such a view would contradict the scriptural teaching of the eternal security of those who are "in Christ" as well as John 3:36 which says of those who disobey the Son that "the wrath of God rests upon" (Greek = "remains upon") them. God's wrath was never removed from them. Those who will be finally lost were never "elect in Christ" (Chapter Seven).

3) Biblical Universalism (premise B) is a *working principle*. As such, it is a general premise *assumed to be true* until, in a particular instance, it becomes evident that we are confronted with one of the exceptions allowed for in the premise.

4) Christian communicators who work with premise A switch the scope of reference when they use such pronouns as "we," "us," and "our." They include all listeners when they proclaim that through Adam's sin "we" are made sinners. They intend to exclude some when they declare that by Christ's obedience "we" are made righteous. The serious inquirer is left with a sense of confusion or a feeling that the good news is not really announced, declared or proclaimed to him or her.

5) If Calvinists can allow that there is no consignment to hell **apart from** individual, final (persistent), willful unbelief and sin on part of the person so condemned, and if Arminians can allow that Christ's atonement accomplished salvation for the elect rather than merely making it a possibility, then progress can be made by Arminians and Calvinists toward a common understanding of the good news. (see Addendum B, page 119).

6) To put the premise of Biblical Universalism into practice is to view every person and treat him or her as one "for whom Christ died" (1 Cor. 8:11) unless and until they give decisive and final evidence to the contrary. The approach of Biblical Universalism breaks down barriers between people. It promotes a feeling of genuine concern and mutual trust. It helps overcome prejudices which arise out of fear because we view others apathetically, or worse still, with suspicion.

The premise of Biblical Universalism is—All persons are elect in Christ except those who the Bible expressly declares will be finally lost. On this basis we are to view all persons as heirs of the kingdom of heaven and to announce and declare to them the good news of what God in Christ has done for **us.** According to Ephesians 2:17 we must preach peace to those who are far off (outside the Covenant) and peace to those who are near (Covenant members).

We must exhort all persons everywhere to respond to this good news by way of repentance, faith and joyful obedience. We must help them, counsel them, and, if need be, warn them to flee the wrath which is sure to come on all who disregard the witness of God in Christ Jesus our Lord.

Because we do not have and never will have final and decisive evidence to the contrary regarding any particular person or group of persons, we must view everyone from the perspective that "[Christ] is the expiation for our sins, and not for ours only but also for the sins of the whole world" (1 John 2:2). We have biblical warrant for respecting all persons as equal children of God and for warning everyone that willful and final refusal to live as a child of God will be just cause for his or her condemnation.

CHAPTER SEVEN

Biblical Particularism

NOT everything that God desires has come to pass. Why this should be so or how this is even possible far exceeds our ability to understand. "How often would I have gathered your children together as a hen gathers her brood under her wings, and you would not!" (Matt. 23:37). "For I have no pleasure in the death of anyone, says the Lord God; so turn, and live" (Ezek. 18:32). God our Savior "desires all men to be saved and to come to the knowledge of the truth" (1 Tim. 2:4). "Not wishing that any should perish, but that all should reach repentance" (2 Peter 3:9).

It is also true that the sacrifice Christ made on the cross has infinite atoning value. That is to say, if all persons were to be saved or even if there were many worlds of people who were to be saved, Christ's sacrifice would not have to be greater. For reasons known only to God, God's purpose, design, intention or plan in salvation is not revealed as being equally extensive as his desire and ability to save. Biblical Particularism addresses only the question of whether God designs, intends, purposes to save all persons.

The obvious sense of the so-called "universalistic" texts just as we find them in our English (and Greek) Bible is confirmed by the combined wisdom of thousands of Christian scholars working for many centuries. These passages speak of an accomplished, certain-to-be-realized salvation, and they do so in reference to all persons (Chapter Two). This is not to say that all persons will be finally saved as Universalists contend. The broader context of Scripture clearly reveals that there are exceptions to these texts (Chapter Three).

39

If, as we have been contending, the Bible speaks of an accomplished, certain-to-be-realized salvation for all persons (with the exception of those who Scripture expressly declares will not be saved), it necessarily follows that all those and only those for whom Christ accomplished salvation will be saved. This teaching is variously called limited, definite or particular atonement.

God's Purpose in Jesus Christ

Besides the fact that a correct reading of the so-called "universalistic" texts implies a particular atonement, we call attention to two other arguments that demonstrate that all those and only those who God intends or decrees to save will be saved:

1) First of all, as Dr. Roger R. Nicole points out (as quoted in Punt, *Unconditional Good News,* page 70), the very words used to describe Christ's work are definite and particular. **Redemption** is Christ's gracious work by which he sets his people free from their sin and eternal death. Has redemption truly occurred if the redeemed sinner remains in his or her sin and will suffer its final consequence? Christ is the **propitiation** for the sins of his people. Propitiation describes how the wrath of God against sinners is removed by way of substitution. Can it be said that God's wrath is removed if those for whom the propitiation is made remain under the wrath of God? Christ's work is one of **reconciliation** between God and the sinner. Has reconciliation occurred as God's work in Christ if those who have been reconciled forever remain at enmity with God?

2) Secondly there are many passages of Scripture that describe the design, intention, purpose, plan, motivation for Christ giving his life on the cross. He would "save his people from their sin" (Matt. 1:21); he gave his life in order that he "should lose nothing of all that" were given to him by the Father (John 6:38, 39); he would lay down his life in order that "they might have life and have it abundantly" (John 10:10, 11); and he gave himself up "for the church" so that he might present the church to himself "holy and without blemish" (Eph. 5:26, 27).

There are some who will not be "saved from their sins," will be finally "lost," will never "have life," and will never become "holy and without blemish." Either the Lord Jesus Christ, to whom "all authority in heaven and on earth has been given" for the express purpose of calling and gathering his people to salvation (Matt. 28:18) is unsuccessful in accomplishing his expressed intention, purpose, design, or plan for these individuals; or, they were never included in the saving purpose of Christ's death. It cannot be the former "Since thou hast given him power over all flesh, to give eternal life to all whom thou hast given him" (John 17:2).

Biblical Universalism accepts the particularism of Scripture, namely, that Christ died only for "his sheep," "his own," "the elect," "the church," or "those given him by the Father" and each one of these is certain to come to salvation in Christ. However, premise B differs from the historic expressions of Calvinism in that it defines "his sheep," "his own", or "the elect," and "those given him by the Father" as *all persons* except those who the Bible expressly declares will be finally lost.

God *loved* the world, and Christ *loved* His church; Christ *died* for all, and He *died* for His sheep; He *gave Himself a ransom* for all, and He *gave Himself a ransom* for many. It is the same love, death and ransom that is described in reference to the all and the sheep; the all and the many; the world and the church. The "particularistic" texts of Scripture and the "universalistic" texts have reference to the **same group** of individuals. They refer to **all persons** except those who throughout their entire life refuse to have God in their knowledge.

The immediate context dictated for the biblical writers the choice between the limited and unlimited phrasing. Because this love, death and ransom was for the benefit of the same group of persons, it can be said that God's gracious redemptive acts were accomplished in behalf of a definite, particular, limited number of persons.

Beyond Logic

The definite or particular view of the atonement has been frowned upon by Arminians not so much because the biblical evidence for it is weak but because they, as well as many Calvinists, draw an unwarranted and unbiblical conclusion from it. Both the proponents and opponents of the doctrine of particular atonement are mistaken when they conclude that this view *necessarily* means that God from eternity determined the ultimate destiny of all persons. Particular atonement, they say, requires that there be a division of humanity into two camps: those elected to salvation "before the foundation of the world" (Eph. 1:4) and those who were eternally rejected.

According to the ordinary rules of reason, if there is a sovereign, unconditional election to salvation of a definite number of persons (less than all) from before the foundation of the world and if Christ made atonement for these and for these only, then there must necessarily be some who were rejected before they came into being. This apparently logical deduction is sometimes called "double predestination."

The picture is further complicated by the fact that the Holy Spirit never fails in his work of renewing the heart, will and mind of those for whom Christ died, giving them the gifts of repentance, faith and obedience. The Father, the Son and the Holy Spirit are one in purpose and work in bringing salvation to God's people.

Therefore one might say that God's not choosing some is tantamount to his rejection of them. The Bible, however, **never** draws that implication and neither may we. In this specific matter Scripture is "splendidly illogical," as A. M. Hunter says. "The opposite of election is not predestination to destruction; it is unbelief—a self-incurred thing" (*The Gospel According to St. Paul*, Westminster, 1966).

The Bible continually stresses that whereas the elect owe their election to the gracious sovereign act of God, the condition of the non-elect results from their individual, willful, final (persistent) unbelief and sin (Chapter Four). The reality of how these two concepts are interrelated is beyond our ability to comprehend. "We should contemplate the evident cause of condemnation in the corrupt nature of humanity—which is closer to us—rather than seek a hidden and utterly incomprehensible cause in God's predestination" (John Calvin, *Institutes*, III, xxiii,8).

God's Sovereignty and Man's Responsibility

Every theological construction or framework which attempts to describe the plan of salvation comes to a certain point where the relationship between God's sovereignty and man's responsibility are not reconcilable to the human mind. The location of that point is not a matter of indifference to be arbitrarily placed where we need it in order to maintain our unexamined assumption. That "certain point" must be located where God's Word forces us to admit it.

Those who will be finally lost (the reprobate) are described in Scripture **in no other way** than those, and only those, who, in addition to their sin in Adam, persist in unbelief and sin, exhibit unbelief, are the agents of unbelief, and perform evil actions throughout their lifetime on earth. They are lost by their own deliberate and inexcusable choice. They will receive that which they have willfully and personally chosen, namely, to depart from God. They are those, and only those, who willfully, decisively and finally reject God's will as it has been made known to them in general revelation (Rom. 1:20; 2:15) or as it was declared to them in special revelation (John 3:18, 5:45).

The Bible never even attempts to explain *the cause* for a person refusing to have God in his or her knowledge. We do not, cannot, and need not know of any reason for this life-long, self-destructive unbelief and sin. God's Word speaks of an election from eternity, and it does not speak of a corresponding rejection from eternity. Biblical Universalism accepts this as the point at which revelation goes beyond human ability to understand. Therefore it does not force the conclusion that mankind is divided into two camps, the elected and the rejected ones.

Because the Bible describes those who are outside of Christ in negative terms, it is best to speak of eternal election in terms of one camp surrounded by "no man's land." It is "no man's land" because no one has a right to be outside of Christ (Matt. 4:10). No one remains there against his or her own will (John 5:40). No one on earth is hopelessly and helplessly consigned there (Rev. 22:17b). No one is there because the gospel has not reached them (Acts 10:34, 35). No one is unjustly there (Acts 13:46). No one is there because God wishes or desires him or her to be there (2 Pet. 3:9). We do not know and Scripture does not tell us why anyone would want to be there or for that matter even how anyone can be there. The Bible speaks of this "no man's land" as an inexplicable darkness, as "the mystery of lawlessness."

A Willful Persistent Choice

We may define the elect as all persons except those who throughout their entire life, personally and willfully refuse to have God in their knowledge. This removes from the comforting truth of a gracious, unconditional, sovereign election unto salvation the horrible thought that certain persons, before they come into existence and totally **apart from** their own personal choice, are consigned, by God's sovereign decree, to eternal death.

The premise of Biblical Universalism underscores the fact that no one rejected on the judgment day will be able to attribute his or her condemnation to God's desire, to the union of all of us with Adam in original sin, to the insufficiency of Christ's atonement, or to the fact that the gospel was never presented to him or her. The condemnation of everyone who is lost will be wholly attributable to himself or herself for having disregarded God's will as it was made known to them (Chapter Four).

Who determines whether someone will be saved or lost? This question has supposedly served as a test to determine whether one is a Calvinist (one who believes that Christ died for a definite number of persons) or an Arminian (one who believes that Christ died for all persons without exception).

Presumably the Calvinist would say it is God who makes the determination, and the Arminian could not deny that each individual person makes the final decision. In the light of what we have said in this chapter, this is no "either—or" situation. For those who are finally lost the Bible reveals no other cause than their own willful, persistent, unbelief and sin. For those who are saved, it is God alone who graciously, sovereignly, elects and saves them.

Biblical Universalism recognizes that the affirming response of faith, repentance, and joyful obedience finds its origin **exclusively** in the sovereign, eternal, electing grace of God apart from any human act. It also teaches that the response of persistent unbelief, indifference or disobedience brings its fatal consequence by way of the "here and now" human decision and is **entirely man's responsibility.**

How can that be? The answer eludes us and believers gratefully recognize that they need not resolve this problem. One merely traces the lines laid out in God's inspired Word.

CHAPTER EIGHT

One Gospel for All

SOME Christians are accused of having two gospels: one for their children and another for the unchurched and unreached. Although it cannot be said that they have two gospels, the accusation has a measure of truth in it. There are those who present the promise of the gospel together with the command to repent and believe to their children on one basis and on a different basis to all other persons.

In the training and nurturing of their children they rely on the covenant promise made with Abraham and his descendants recognizing that "If you are Christ's, then you are Abraham's offspring, heirs according to promise" (Gal. 3:29). They perceive their children to be heirs of God, under grace, elect in Christ, until or unless those children give decisive and final evidence to the contrary.

Before there is evidence of conversion they teach their children that they are not their own but that they belong, body and soul, to their faithful Savior who has fully satisfied for all their sins. These children are nurtured in the assurance that God loves them so much that he sent his Son to die for them. They believe that there is biblical warrant for so regarding **all** their children even though, as painful as the thought is, some of their children may not be numbered among God's elect (see Addendum A).

Urgently and prayerfully they teach their children that they must repent of their sins, believe in Jesus Christ as their Savior and live as children of God. Ideally this loving concern continues, no matter how grievously rebuffed, as long as the parent and child live. This is so, among other reasons, because these parents recognize the dire consequences if their children should finally "refuse to have God in their knowledge."

Such a perspective is consistent with God's way of relating to mankind in creation, in establishing his covenant with Abraham and in confirming it with Israel. God's people and their descendants enjoyed God's fellowship and blessing unless they willfully and finally refuse to have God in their knowledge (Chapter Six).

Other Sheep

A similar concern, interest in, and willingness to sacrifice for, will be engendered for the unchurched and unreached only when we learn to view them as heirs of God, elect in Christ, those for whom Christ died (Premise B, Page 2). The "universalistic" passages provide the biblical warrant for so regarding all persons even though some of them may not be numbered among God's elect.

When Jesus ". . . saw the crowds, he had compassion for them, because they were harassed and helpless, like sheep without a shepherd" (Matt. 9:36). We will so view the masses of mankind and have true compassion for them when we view them as sheep who belong to Christ's fold.

It is with this perspective that we ought to identify with all persons, declaring the good news of what God in Christ **has done for us,** urgently and prayerfully entreating them to repent of their sin, be reconciled to God, and live as those who have been made free in Christ. We must do so because we recognize the dire consequences if they should refuse "to have God in their knowledge."

Christians who view their children as children of God, unless or until they refuse to have God in their knowledge, are suspected of having two gospels—one for their own children and another for all non-Christians. Those Christians who view their own children (at least in theory) as lost, outside of Christ, unless or until they make a credible confession of faith, are credited with having one gospel which they proclaim on the same basis to all persons.

In terms of the two perspectives A and B (Page 2), it can be said that some Christians work with premise B in communicating the good news to their own children, and they use premise A in bringing the good news to all other persons. Other Christians in theory (if not in practice) use only premise A.

The point is that there are not two gospels, one for church people and another for the unchurched and unreached. Neither are there two different bases for announcing and declaring the good news together with the command to repent and believe. The promise of the gospel together with the command to repent and believe "ought to be announced and declared *without differentiating or discriminating*, to all nations and people, to whom God in his good pleasure sends the gospel" (Canons of Dort II, 5, emphasis added).

The Gospel is Good News

Because there is only one gospel that is to be proclaimed on the same basis to all persons without "differentiating or discriminating," we must make a choice between premise A and B. We must either work with the traditional mind-set A—that all persons are outside of Christ except those who the Bible expressly declares will be saved; or acknowledge B—that all persons are elect in Christ except those who the Bible expressly declares will be finally lost.

Premise A provides no warrant for declaring or announcing "good news" to all persons in general or to any person in particular until or unless they give evidence of conversion. This premise, if consistently applied, provides a basis only for "bad news" coupled with a good suggestion or prescription to bring about a desired result. With premise A the burden of the church is to tell all nations and every person that they are lost, they are condemned, they are on the way to hell, but if they believe they will be saved.

In the preceding chapters we presented the biblical evidence for working with premise B, that "As in Adam all die, so also in Christ shall all be made alive" (1 Cor. 15:22), except those who the Bible expressly declares will not inherit the kingdom of heaven. This premise provides the biblical warrant for a positive gospel of acceptance and affirmation for all persons. There is scriptural warrant for respecting all persons as equal children of God, as sheep who belong to the fold of Christ. We have the joyous task of proclaiming God's ultimate jubilee to the whole world.

Necessary Valid Warnings

This does not mean that regardless of circumstances we must greet everyone "with a holy kiss" and that we are obligated willy-nilly to assure them that God loves them and Christ died for them. When those with whom we come into contact are acting like dogs and swine we are not to give that which is holy to them nor throw our pearls before them (Matt. 7:6). Biblical Universalism does, however, profoundly affect the way in which and the reasons for which we find it necessary in certain circumstances to withhold our brotherly or sisterly embrace from them.

It may even be that due to their actions we must withdraw acceptance from members of the church and do so through official discipline. "If he refuses to listen even to the church, let him be to you as a Gentile and a tax collector" (Matt. 18:17). Persons living in flagrant disobedience to God's revealed will have the right to be warned in the strongest possible way that if they willfully *persist* in their unbelief and sin they will find the gates of heaven closed to them.

We are never given the decisive and unmistakable evidence that a particular person will continue to live in willful unbelief and sin without ever repenting of that sin. Therefore we may never draw the conclusion concerning any particular person or group of persons that they are outside of Christ.

If ever there appeared to be such decisive and final evidence, it was in the life of apostle Paul before his conversion. But even while doing many things "contrary to the name of Jesus," Paul was one of those whom God through Christ had reconciled unto himself.

Looking back upon his life Paul said that God "had set me apart before I was born, and had called me through his grace" (Gal. 1:16). If such a person as Paul was elect in Christ before he was born we ought to assume every sinner is an elect child of God unless and until we have final evidence to the contrary. Paul acknowledges that he is the chief example of God's grace.

"For the Day Will Disclose It"

God alone can and will decide who has finally and decisively refused "to have God in their knowledge." That decision will not be manifest until "the last day." "If anyone hears my sayings and does not keep them, I do not judge him, for I did not come to judge the world but to save the world. He who rejects me and does not receive my sayings has a judge; the word that I have spoken will be his judge on the last day" (John 12:47, 48).

Until that "last day" we must continue with the perspective that "In Christ God was reconciling the world to himself, not counting their trespasses against them, and entrusting to us the message of reconciliation" (II Cor. 5:19). Therefore we declare to one and all "The word of truth, the gospel [good news] of your salvation" (Eph. 1:13).

There is biblical warrant for regarding and insisting that all persons regard themselves as equal children of God. We must exhort all persons to "consider [themselves] dead to sin and alive to God in Christ Jesus" (Rom. 6:11), warning them that willful and persistent refusal to do so will be the just cause of their condemnation.

The practical application of how we must communicate this "one gospel" to all nations and to individual persons requires the leading of the Spirit and a finely tuned sense of Christian discernment with which we must become more familiar.

We undoubtedly will find that the attitude we cultivate toward ourselves and toward those we seek to reach with the gospel is much more important than the words we speak or the techniques we use. This attitude must be formed by accepting ourselves and every person we meet as equally children of God, beloved of God for Christ's sake. "If I speak with the tongues of men and of angels, but have not love, I am a noisy gong or a clanging cymbal" (1 Cor. 13:1).

CHAPTER NINE

Unconditional Good News

IT is not by living in obedience to God that a person becomes a Christian. But a Christian must live in obedience to God. D. Martyn Lloyd-Jones calls our attention to this when he says: "We are not told in the Sermon on the Mount, 'Live like this and you will become Christian'; rather we are told, 'Because you are Christian live like this.'" He goes on to say that **all the appeals to ethical conduct** in every New Testament epistle are based on this same presumption, namely, that the reader has a new standing with God in Christ. (*Studies in the Sermon on the Mount*, Wm. B. Eerdmans Publishing Co., 1959, Vol. I, pp. 17, 23, 24.)

A person's new standing with God in Christ requires that he or she must live differently. Dr. John Murray uses the following analogy to help us understand this basic truth: "To say to the slave who has not been emancipated, 'Do not behave as a slave' is to mock his enslavement. But to say the same to the slave who has been set free is the necessary appeal to put into effect the privileges and rights of his liberation" (*The Epistle to the Romans*, Wm. B. Eerdmans Publishing Co., 1959, I, p. 227).

Presumed To Be

The New Testament writers assume that their readers are no longer slaves of sin. The readers are presumed to have been set free from the power of sin, and they are commanded to put into effect the privileges and rights of the liberty they have in Christ. What they are required, expected, commanded **to do** is based on what they **are presumed to be** in Christ. "Let not sin reign in your mortal bodies" (*to do*) because "you are not under law but under grace" (*presumed to be*) (Rom. 6:12, 14). The readers are not to live after the flesh but according to the Spirit (*to do*) because "you are not in the flesh, you are in the spirit" (*presumed to be*) (Rom. 8:9). They must put "away falsehood" (*to do*) because "we are members one of another" (*presumed to be*) (Eph. 4:25). "Set your minds on things that are above" (*to do*) because "your life is hid with Christ in God" (*presumed to be*) (Col. 3:2, 3).

These are not prescriptions or suggested ways to gain a new standing with God in Christ. It is not by "putting away falsehood" that they will become "members one of another" and so on. The appeal to do differently is based on the presumption that the readers are new creations in Christ.

Lloyd-Jones correctly observes that **all the appeals to ethical conduct** in every New Testament epistle are based on this same presumption. These appeals to ethical conduct are summed up in the familiar trio —repent, believe and obey. These calls to new obedience in Christ can be called "gospel demands" (that is, demands that arise out of the "good news"). They are based on the assumption that the one who reads or hears is a new creature in Christ.

This poses a very important question. How far does this presumption of being "in Christ" extend? Most of the New Testament letters were addressed to churches. The human authors had no way of knowing who were genuine Christians among those church members. Were the gospel demands made of all members of the church? Were only those who had made a confession of faith in Christ presumed to have new standing in Christ? Are the New Testament "appeals to ethical conduct" to be announced and declared to persons who are not members of the church? Is it left up to each individual to determine whether or not the gospel demands have validity and appeal for him or her?

The fact that the gospel demands are inseparably related to a person's **presumed** new standing in Christ forces us to choose among three possibilities:

Possibility #1—The gospel demands are imposed only on a limited number of individuals, that is, those who are presumed to be new creations in Christ (whoever they may be). These demands are not placed on the rest of humanity.

This cannot be the answer because all the appeals to ethical conduct are addressed to every person who reads the Bible or hears it preached. "Let not sin therefore reign in your mortal bodies" (Rom. 6:12) is God's will for everyone who hears. Every human being is obligated to put away falsehood and speak the truth with his neighbor (Eph. 4:25). All who are confronted with the Word of God are obligated to "Set [their] mind on the things that are above" (Col. 3:2).

The gospel demands are not limited to certain individuals: "But now he commands all men everywhere to repent" (Acts 17:30); "Him we proclaim, warning every man and teaching every man in all wisdom, that we may present every man mature in Christ" (Col. 1:28).

Possibility #2—The same demands, requirements, come to all persons but for a limited number of persons these demands are based on their presumed new standing in Christ. The same obedience is required of all other persons on some other basis—perhaps on the basis of their having been created in the image of God.

The difficulty with this answer is that it is impossible to demonstrate from the Bible that there is a different basis for making these demands of some people than for others. There is only one gospel and it is to be proclaimed on the same basis to all persons. (Chapter Eight).

Possibility #3—All the gospel demands are addressed to all persons and find their validity and appeal on the same basis.

God "Commands All Men Everywhere"

The over-all message of Scripture that—All persons are elect in Christ except those who the Bible expressly declares will be lost (Premise B, Page 2)—provides the biblical warrant for this third possibility. We may and must assume that every one we approach with the gospel has a new standing with God in Christ unless or until we have decisive and final evidence to the contrary.

The Old Testament was entrusted to the Hebrews. The New Testament epistles were addressed to the churches. In neither instance is it to be understood that the good news is limited to either one nation or to the community of believers. The church is the "pillar and bulwark of the truth" so that it may be preserved from generation to generation, but the "mystery of our religion" is to be "preached among the nations, believed on in the world" (1 Tim. 3:15, 16).

Although the Epistles were sent to the churches, their message is God's Word to all persons. "In the Bible God is wrestling with the world, persuading, reproving, admonishing, beseeching the various peoples of the world to accept the truth and be reconciled to God" (J. H. Bavinck, *The Impact of Christianity on the Non-Christian World*, Wm. B. Eerdmans Publishing Co., 1948, p. 139).

"This promise, together with the command to repent and believe, ought to be announced and declared without differentiating or discriminating to all nations and people, to whom God in his good pleasure sends the gospel" (*Canons of Dort*, II, 5). The gospel demands are not reserved for a limited number of persons. They are demanded of everyone to whom the gospel comes.

Consider this demand which must be made of everyone who hears the gospel: "Be reconciled to God!" (2 Cor. 5:20). The command is not that they must reconcile themselves to God. The verb is passive. There is no human participation in reconciliation. "All this is from God, who through Christ reconciled us to himself" (vs: 18). Reconciliation is God's act of "not counting their trespasses against them" (vs. 19). The "message of reconciliation" (vs. 19) is a message (announcement, declaration) of something that God **has done** through Christ. It is not a promise of something God **will do** when and if one believes.

Reconciliation, therefore, may not be presented as a prescription or a suggestion to the sinner informing him or her of what they must do to move God to "not count their sins against them." To "be reconciled to God" is to rest in (not reject) the good news that God has not counted your trespasses against you.

On the one hand "Be reconciled to God!" can be demanded only of those who are presumed to have been reconciled to God through Christ. On the other hand we must demand this of every person in every nation.

The resolution of this problem is found in premise B—All persons are elect in Christ except those who the Bible expressly declares will be lost. "In Christ God was reconciling *the world* to himself, not counting their trespasses against them" (2 Cor. 5:19, emphasis added). If this is understood as a "generalization" as it must be (Chapter Five), then we have biblical warrant for presuming that everyone we approach with the gospel has been reconciled to

God through Christ unless and until we have final and decisive evidence to the contrary. We need not hesitate to be ambassadors for Christ demanding of all persons everywhere that they "be reconciled to God," that is, that they do not reject the good news that their transgressions are not counted against them.

Having said this we must immediately point out that all the gospel demands serve a two-fold purpose. They are intended to bring to expression and to maturity the new life that is presumed to be in those to whom we bring the gospel (the good news). At the same time these demands serve as a test to determine whether in fact such new life is present. If what is demanded **never** takes place, then, and only then, we can conclude that this particular person is one of the exceptions allowed for in our premise.

Absolute Certainty?

There are those who say that promises, demands and announce-ments of good news cannot be made to any specific individual or group of persons on the basis of an assumption or generalization. They say that person-specific announcements, promises and de-mands can be made *only* on the basis of a universalization (which necessarily applies to every person without any exceptions) or a perception that a particular person or group is involved. If these are the only two possibilities (and they do appear to be born of flawless logic), then we must decide on which of these two bases we may ever say to any person or group "Christ died for you," or "Be reconciled to God!"; that is, God reconciled you to himself through Christ's death so that your transgressions are not counted against you.

On the basis of God's Word we rule out universalization (Chap-ter Three). We then need evidence that a particular person or group is **necessarily** included in God's work of reconciliation before we can say to them "Christ died for you." What kind of evidence must this be? It cannot be simply a confession of faith in Christ together with a lifestyle that appears to be consistent with this confession. There are false professors of Christ living apparently godly lives. We can **never** be certain that such a perception corresponds with reality.

The evidence we need is some objective, absolute, verifiable proof or certainty that this particular person or group actually is among those who have been reconciled to God through Christ. This kind of "proof" is **never** available to us, not even for those professing Christians who are closest and dearest to us. To insist on universalization or such special evidence as the **only** bases for a person-specific announcement precludes ever saying to any individual or congregation "Christ died for you."

That we are **not** so limited in saying "Christ died for you" is evident from such passages as 1 Corinthians 15:3 "For I delivered to you as of first importance what I also received, that Christ died for our sins in accordance with the Scriptures." Paul neither based this declaration on "universalization" nor did he base it on some recognizable, absolutely certain evidence gained from the lives of those to whom he declared it. Paul specifically says that he "delivered to" them something he had received long before he set foot in the city of Corinth, namely, the message of reconciliation— "Christ died for our sins." This is the biblically warranted presumption with which we may work unless and until we have decisive and final evidence to the contrary.

The gospel is an announcement of an objective state of affairs for all the elect. The gospel is good news. One cannot exhort, entreat or conditionally offer "news." This is not a clever play on the English word "news." To offer the gospel conditionally is to make the gospel a new law, a prescription with requirements for those to whom the gospel comes, and the whole problem of the impotency of the law is revived, that is, the problem of having to "do something" to attain salvation (Chapter Ten).

What must be exhorted, entreated, is an appropriate **response** to the gospel. The gospel is not a prescription, a proposal—If you "believe" ("repent," "obey") then Christ will "save" ("redeem," "die for") you. The gospel is the good news that—Christ has "redeemed" ("saved," "died for") you, therefore you must "believe" ("repent," "obey"). This "good news"together with the command to repent and believe can be announced and declared to all nations and people without differentiating or discriminating only on the assumption that all those to whom the gospel is sent have been reconciled to God through Christ.

CHAPTER TEN

Isn't Faith Necessary?

ETERNAL death is the fate of those **and only those** who, in addition to their sin in Adam, throughout their entire life, choose by their indifference or rebelliousness to persist in unbelief and sin (Chapter Four). This is obviously consistent with the view that—All are elect in Christ except those who the Bible expressly declares will be finally lost.

But the Bible not only warns against the serious consequences of persistent unbelief and sin, it places as great an emphasis—if not greater—on the urgency and necessity of believing. Those who would be saved must "repent," "believe," "obey," "come to Christ," "follow him" and so on. There appears to be some prerequisite, condition or requirement for a person to be saved. If nothing else, isn't faith necessary?

There is a legitimate distinction between salvation considered objectively and salvation considered subjectively. Salvation considered objectively is a past event, accomplished on the cross by Christ for all the elect. It is this objective salvation which we have in mind when in this chapter we ask the question "Isn't Faith Necessary?"

Salvation can also be considered subjectively and therefore the Bible also speaks of those who "are being saved" (1 Cor. 1:18). Subjective salvation is the knowledge and comfort that one gains and enjoys by accepting "the gospel [good news] of [his or her] salvation" (Eph. 1:13). We shall speak more of the distinction between objective and subjective salvation in Chapter Fifteen.

Because the church has always worked with premise A—All persons are outside of Christ except those who the Bible explicitly

57

declares will be saved—the history of theology can be traced in terms of how the church has defined the "exceptions" to this premise, that is, those who will be saved. Whatever it is that distinguishes those who will be saved from those who will be finally lost was considered to be a prerequisite, condition or requirement for salvation.

"With Men This is Impossible"

A great variety of such "conditions" have been proposed. Today Christians generally hold that all persons are outside of Christ and are subject to eternal death except those who make and maintain a personal commitment of faith. There is little agreement, however, about how it is possible for those who are sinful by nature, unable in their own strength to believe, to fulfill any condition or requirement for their salvation.

Some claim that even after the Fall into sin certain remnants of original righteousness remain in all sinners. These traces of original goodness enable the sinner to make the positive decision to believe the gospel when it is presented to him or her.

Others say that through the Fall the descendants of Adam lost **all** ability to contribute even the least bit toward their own restoration. God, they say, provides every sinner equal access to the grace of salvation. This "equal access" is provided either: by a seed of grace planted in every sinner's heart enabling them to respond favorably to the gospel and thereby receive saving grace; or, by an enabling grace which always accompanies the Word preached; or, by a "foreseen" faith. God in eternity "foresaw" those who would believe when the gospel would be presented to them, and on this basis chose those individuals to salvation. There is no agreement among evangelical Christians as to which of these views, or the myriad variations of them, is the correct biblical perspective.

Calvinists do not agree that God provides "equal access" to the grace of salvation. God, according to his sovereign, incomprehensible, gracious good pleasure, has unconditionally chosen a definite, limited number of persons to salvation. By a miracle of sovereign grace he creates faith in their hearts. The rest of mankind, according to God's just judgment, is passed by to suffer the consequence of their sin in Adam as well as all their other sins.

Reacting to the thought of a "limited" number, some Calvinists hold that all persons are both elect and reprobate in Christ. They do not admit the apparent consequence of such a teaching that all persons would be saved. Others find a problem in the concept of a "definite" number chosen to salvation. They conclude there is an *essential* "correlation" between faith and God's mercy, a correlation established by God himself. Consequently there is no election to salvation before the actual (existential) moment of exercised faith and there is no "definite" number of persons chosen to receive God's mercy.

"All the king's horses and all the king's men" cannot put this puzzle back together again. This great variety of proposed solutions to the problem of a sinner's inability to respond to God's "offer" of salvation exist because salvation is *erroneously* thought to be conditional. The indisputable **fact** that all who believe in the Lord Jesus Christ will be saved is mistakenly understood to mean that faith is the one condition, prerequisite, or requirement that sinners must meet in order to be saved.

"With God All Things Are Possible"

The Bible neither stipulates any condition or requirement for salvation nor does it indicate how man in sin is capable of fulfilling such a condition. Because these are not found in God's Word, each theological tradition suggests a different answer. Salvation is not conditional. Salvation is God's work, divine in its origin, divine in its execution and divine in its fulfillment. "Therefore, if any one is in Christ, he is a new creation; the old has passed away, behold, the new has come. All this is from God, who through Christ reconciled us to himself" (2 Cor. 5:17, 18).

God's people are chosen in Christ Jesus before the foundation of the world. They are redeemed by the blood of Christ. In accordance with this election in Christ the Holy Spirit works the miracle of grace in them renewing their heart, will, and mind, making them "a new creation."

This election does not take place because they already are, in some small measure, what God requires them to be. They are chosen in order that they may become what God wants them to be—"Even as he chose us in him before the foundation of the world, that we should be holy and blameless before him" (Eph. 1:4).

The difficult questions are not "Who will be saved" and "Why are they saved?" The unresolvable question is "Why are any lost?" The Bible provides no answer to this last question other than the willful and persistent unbelief and sin of those who will be finally lost. (See Chapters Four and Seven.)

Faith does not bring about a new standing in our relationship to the sovereign, eternal, electing grace of God. Faith is the fruit of the sovereign electing grace of God in the believer's heart, illuminating the mind, renewing the will, creating new life.

Faith is a matter of resting in, clinging to, appropriating with a personal intensity the good news of God's Word regarding our new standing in Christ. This "new standing" was determined apart from any faith, act, or attitude of ours by one "who saved us and called us with a holy calling, not in virtue of our works but in virtue of his own purpose and grace which he gave us in Christ Jesus ages ago" (2 Tim. 1:9).*

Saved by Grace

But what about all the urgent demands to repent, believe, obey, to walk worthily of our calling, to do good works, and so on, that are found throughout the Bible? Are not these conditions, prerequisites, requirements for salvation? At the very least, isn't a personal faith in Jesus Christ necessary for salvation?

The question that must be answered is this, "Why is it absolutely necessary for all those who hear the gospel to 'believe in him whom he has sent'?" Is it because this is the one prerequisite, condition, requirement without which God is either unable or unwilling to save sinners? What does it mean that we are "justified by faith?"

---

*There are those who say that the "dynamic relation of eternity to time" resolves the problem of whether it is God's sovereign election, the sinner's faith, or both, that are involved in determining our new standing with God in Christ. They say God's electing act is eternal —it is before, during and after man's decision to believe. Thus we need not speak about which is first. In fact, they say, there is no election until the moment faith is exercised. Our reply is that the difficulty is not one of timing at all. It is a question of whether God sovereignly initiates and creates new life in those whom he will. Whether this action on God's part occurs before or during the sinner's decision to believe is irrelevant.

There are two aspects to these questions that must be considered before we can give a direct answer to them:

1) **First:** When Paul says that we are "justified by faith," he does so because many of his readers considered themselves justified by keeping the law. God's **grace** for them consisted in the fact that God gave them his law, so that by keeping the law they could earn acceptance with him. Had Paul used the expression "we are justified by grace," his readers would associate that grace with their having been given God's law. That would be the very opposite of Paul's intention: "For we hold that a man is justified by faith apart from works of law" (Rom. 3:29).

There are **only two ways** to be "justified" or accounted righteous. Either by deeds done in perfect obedience to the law, or by receiving righteousness as a gift of God's grace. "Justification by faith" is too often presented as if it were some middle way between "justification by works" and "justification by grace."

To envision "justification by faith" as anything other than "justification by grace" is to distort the biblical teaching of "justification by faith." "There is no distinction," everyone who is justified is "justified by his grace as a gift, through the redemption which is in Christ Jesus" (Rom. 3:24).

To be "saved" or "justified by faith" is **nothing more or less** than to be "saved" or "justified by grace" and to so understand it removes any thought of conditionality. It is "through faith" that we understand we are saved "by grace."

We are saved by faith (and receive other blessings also by faith) only in the sense that to do anything other than to believe is to continue in unbelief. Barth is correct in saying, "If faith seeks to be more than a vacuum, it is unbelief." "That is why it depends on faith, in order that the promise may rest on grace" (Rom. 4:16).

The same can be said about works. We are justified by works. "You see that a man is justified by works and not by faith alone" (James 2:24). Not that these works any more than our faith are a condition or prerequisite for salvation, but only in the sense that to refuse or neglect to perform good works is to live in unbelief. Such willful, persistent unbelief and sin is the prescription, condition, prerequisite for condemnation.

2) **Second:** Many of the passages which speak of faith, repentance or some other form of obedience to the will of God are *descriptive*, not *prescriptive*. That is to say, they are a description of the actual situation. They are not a prescription for bringing

about a desired result. They are a statement of fact, not a conditional offer.

"For God so loved the world that he gave his only Son, that whoever believes in him should not perish but have eternal life" (John 3:16). This is often read to mean that "believing" is a condition or prescription for salvation. The text says no such thing. This text, and many others like it, is a description of the actual situation which pertains to those who believe. It is a significant, comforting, and useful description "Whoever believes in him" shall "not perish but have eternal life." This text does not say, and the Bible **never** says, they "have eternal life" **because** they believe in him.

There is a prescription, requirement, condition for one to be finally lost. John 3:18 says, "He who believes in him is not condemned; he who does not believe is condemned already, **because** he has not believed in the name of the only Son of God". Significantly, this verse does **not** say that one is "not condemned" *because* "he believed in him;" but it does say that one "is condemned . . . *because* he has not believed" (emphasis added). The first part of the verse is descriptive, the second part is prescriptive. Salvation is by grace, damnation is by works. In precisely so far as salvation is conditional it is not of grace.

"As in Adam . . . So Also in Christ"

That salvation is exclusively God's work completed for us in Christ, and is not conditioned by some essential human act to establish us in the state of grace, is seen in the analogy between Adam and Christ in Romans 5:12-21. Just as no individualized personal activity is required for Adam's sin to be charged to those whom he represented, so also no individualized personal activity is necessary to transfer Christ's righteousness (the miracle of grace) to those joined to him. The headship of Adam and of Christ is due to a real (not a potential or possible) unity between them and the persons they represent.

"By one man's [Adam's] disobedience many were made [constituted] sinners." There was no additional, self-determined act necessary on the part of those who were joined with him in order to make them sinners. "So by one man's [Christ's] obedience many will be made [constituted] righteous" (Rom. 5:19).

The fact that the sin of Adam is the sin of those represented by him without any further activity on the part of those represented by him, is held up before us in Romans 5:12 through 21 as the parallel to the fact that the righteousness of Christ is the righteousness of those represented by Christ without any further activity on the part of those represented by him. Theologians have referred to this as the "immediate imputation" of Adam's sin and of Christ's righteousness.

Although we have little difficulty accepting the immediate imputation of Adam's sin, we hesitate to accept its parallel—the immediate imputation of the righteousness of Christ. The later seems to make faith unnecessary. Isn't a personal faith in Jesus Christ necessary for salvation?

A Required Response

The answer is an unqualified **yes** for everyone who hears the gospel. Everyone to whom the gospel is meaningfully presented must repent, believe and begin to walk in accordance with God's will or they will not be saved. Urgent demands to repent, believe and obey are found throughout the Bible.

But we must pursue the question "Why are faith and these other acts of obedience *essential* for those who hear the gospel?" It is not because these acts of obedience collectively or the act of faith in particular is the required condition, prerequisite or prescription for salvation. The necessity of repentance, faith and obedience arises from the fact that for those who refuse to so respond to the good news thereby refuse to obey the will of God as it is made known to them.

In the very nature of the case, all the demands to repent, believe in the Lord Jesus Christ and live in joyful obedience through him are addressed only to responsible persons who are confronted with the gospel. For these persons faith is **absolutely necessary** and unbelief is damnable. To reject or remain indifferent to the gospel is to reject the will of God. Such rejection leaves those who hear all the more "without excuse" and if persisted in throughout one's life will end in eternal death.

What human decision can have real significance if the righteousness of Christ is ours by immediate imputation without any personal, individual, human attitude or act that is essential to our being made righteous? If by this question one means, "What human decision can be *instrumental* in determining one's eternal weal or woe?"—the answer of Biblical Universalism is that it is only the negative decision to disregard, disbelieve or remain indifferent to the will of God that is pictured in the Bible as having a **causal** relationship to eternal woe.

Our conclusion is this: it is the decision of persistent (final) unbelief and disobedience which is the cause, or an essential element (condition, requirement or prescription), for God's wrath to be *carried out* against all those who will be finally lost. There is, however, no human act or attitude of faith which is essential for the miracle of grace to occur. Here again we face truth which is beyond human ability to comprehend. It is the same point we reached in Chapter Seven. With your indulgence I ask you to again read the concluding two paragraphs of Chapter Seven (Page 44).

CHAPTER ELEVEN

Infant Salvation

MANY Christians believe that all who die in infancy will be saved. There is little agreement on the biblical basis for this belief. For the most part the church has delicately avoided this subject in its official statements of belief.

In this discussion we use the expression "those who die in infancy" to include those who are mentally incapable and never attain a status of moral accountability. God alone can determine at what point persons become morally accountable for their response to the revelation that God has given of himself to them.

Throughout the centuries the church has accepted the view that —All persons are outside of Christ except those who the Bible expressly declares will be saved. This assumption has led to the commonly held belief that there is an *essential* willful human act, attitude, decision or commitment of faith which must be met for the miracle of grace to occur (Chapter Ten). If there is such a condition or prerequisite for salvation which only a mature, self-determining person can meet, then there must be some other way for those who die in infancy to be saved.

Every Person Deserves to be Lost

Some Christians claim that infants who die are saved on the basis of their **innocency.** Those incapable of moral decision, it is said, are innocent and consequently cannot be penalized. This overlooks the biblical teaching concerning original sin.

Other Christians appeal to **sentimentality.** We cannot find it in ourselves to subject any such infant to eternal death. Therefore we need not think that God could or would do so.

This reasoning is less convincing when we realize that we cannot find it in ourselves to subject any person to eternal death. It is, however, God's holiness, majesty and truth that is violated by sin and must be satisfied. This is a far different standard than mere human sentiment.

Still others say that all such infants, by virtue of their creation in God's image, are both **children of God and of infinite value.** Therefore God will not permit any human being to be finally lost. As appealing as these thoughts are, the Bible does not teach that all human beings are children of God and have infinite value (Chapter Three).

A biblical doctrine of the salvation of all who die in infancy must reckon with the following truths:

1) "We were by nature children of wrath, like the rest of mankind" (Eph. 2:3). The language of the *Belgic Confession*, Art. XV, appears to be strongly worded, but it has stood the test of time and it accurately reflects the teaching of the Bible:

> Through the disobedience of Adam original sin is extended to all mankind; which is a corruption of the whole nature and a hereditary disease, wherewith infants in their mothers womb are infected—and is so vile and abominable in the sight of God that it is sufficient to condemn all mankind.

2) Secondly, the truth, righteousness, and holiness of God must be maintained. This requires that the sentence of condemnation must be carried out unless the sovereign grace of God intervenes to remove the iniquity and sin in which all infants are conceived and born (Psalm 51:5).

Therefore the benefits of Christ's sacrifice must be applied to those who die in infancy if they are to be saved. This alone can remove their guilt, renew them in righteousness and so equip them to rejoice in, serve and praise their maker.

3) A third consideration is that the application of the redemption purchased by Christ must take place prior to their death. Any doctrine which teaches a period of probation for infants after death, so that they may choose to accept Jesus Christ as their savior, not

only engages in extra-biblical speculation, it also concedes that infants *as infants* cannot be saved.

Before they can be saved, according to the *post mortem* (after death) probation view, infants must be mature enough to voluntarily accept the benefits of salvation. They cannot be saved as immature infants. Although this view does not say that all who die in infancy are finally lost, it does not give assurance that such infants will be saved.

ALL ARE ELECT IN CHRIST EXCEPT . . .

The so-called "universalistic" texts of Scripture speak of an actual, certain-to-be-realized salvation in relationship to all persons (Chapter Two). The only exceptions that we may allow are those which are revealed to us by the Bible itself. The Bible nowhere excludes any class of infants, either baptized or unbaptized, born in Christian or heathen lands, born of believing or unbelieving parents, from redemption in Christ.

The **official** elucidation (Page 22) reflects the truth of Scripture, namely, that God **never** consigns anyone to eternal death solely on the basis of that person's sin in Adam, **apart from** willful, persistent unbelief and sin on the part of the person so condemned. From this it necessarily follows that all who die before they are capable of such willful, persistent, unbelief and sin are saved.

"Then as one man's trespass led to condemnation for all men, so one man's act of righteousness leads to acquittal and life for all men" (Rom. 5:18). It is the Bible and the Bible **alone** that may make exceptions to either the first or the second "all men" of this verse. We have no more right to exclude those who die in infancy from the second "all men" of this text than we have the right to exclude them from the first "all men."

Objections Answered

There are those who question the teaching of the salvation of all who die in infancy because we have the account of the death of the "little ones" of Korah, Dathan, and Abiram (Num. 16:27-33), and the family of Achan (Josh. 8:24-26). The Bible, however, does not tell us that these deaths were an expression of God's *eternal* wrath. In fact, the Bible forbids us to say that God held these children accountable for the sin committed by their parents.

Adam represented all persons. Therefore his descendants "were constituted sinners" (Rom. 5:19) by his disobedience. In all other instances the Bible forbids us to think that children will be held accountable for the sins committed by their parents. "The soul that sins shall die. The son shall not suffer for the iniquity of the Father, nor the father suffer for the iniquity of the son" (Ezek. 18:20). The eighteenth chapter of Ezekiel is a vehement denial of the possibility that God would demand payment from children for the sin committed by their parents.

This is not to deny that children often experience the effects of their parents' sin. "Because by this deed you have utterly scorned the Lord, the child that is born to you shall die" (2 Sam. 12:14). However, the death of children as a consequence of the sins of their parents is not evidence that these children pay for the sins of their parents and suffer eternal death (see 2 Sam. 12:23).

One of the consequences of parents' sin is that frequently their children imitate that sin. When God visits "the iniquity of the fathers upon the children to the third and four generation" (Exod. 20:5), it is indeed the "iniquity" that is so visited, not the penalty or payment for that iniquity. Each person is held accountable for his or her own sin. The fact that children suffer the *effects* of the sins of their parents cannot be used as an argument against the view that all who die in infancy are saved.

Another objection raised against the teaching that all who die in infancy are saved is that such a teaching implies that all infants without exception are elect in Christ. This is not a valid conclusion. The only valid conclusion that can be drawn from the death of an infant is that this particular infant will not be among those who willfully and persistently refused to have God in their knowledge (Chapter Four).

Conclusion

If God has revealed himself to be the kind of God who **never** consigns any person to everlasting damnation [hell] **apart from** willful, persistent unbelief and sin on the part of the person so condemned (see the "elucidation," page 22), then we give occasion for "the enemies of God to blaspheme" when we allow even the *possibility* that some babies "a span long" may be cast into hell.

It is only premise B that can, in complete harmony with its basic principles, claim a biblical basis for the salvation of all who die in infancy. Among the redeemed in heaven there will be a countless number of infants who were taken from this earth without ever having willfully rejected God's revelation of himself. They will be eternally praising God for the electing love of the Father which gave them the right to eternal glory, for the cleansing blood of the Son which removed from them the stain of sin and gave them the gift of immortal life, and for the sanctifying work of the Holy Spirit which made them fit inhabitants of heaven.

CHAPTER TWELVE

The Need for Self-Esteem

EVERY person has a deep need for recognition from others and a hunger for self-esteem. This need and hunger are not the inventions of secular humanism or modern psychological theories. This desire for recognition and need for self-esteem find their roots in the fact that we have been created in the image of God who does all things for his own glory.

Recognition from others and self-esteem are among the strongest motivating forces. Satan was wise and subtle enough to make an appeal to them when he tempted our first parents, Adam and Eve, to sin—"You will be like God" (Gen. 3:5).

Satan appealed to something that was good and tempted our first parents to corrupt it. Recognition from others and hunger for self-esteem must have been good in themselves, otherwise Satan could not have made his appeal to them in God's sinless creatures.

Corrupted self-esteem can be called negative self-esteem or sinful pride. Self-esteem (properly understood) has a great potential for good and therefore, when appealed to for evil purposes or distorted into sinful pride, it has a great potential for evil.

It is understandable that the Bible is vehement in its denunciation of corrupted self-esteem. One would be hard pressed to know of any evil that has been more pervasive and done more harm than sinful human pride.

Biblical Guidelines

Self-esteem is not to be rejected. It must be restored to its God-given role by the renewing power of the Holy Spirit according to the following biblical guidelines:

1) A positive self-image is a biblically defined view of oneself as a child of God. Fully that and never anything more than that.

2) It is only by means of an actual, vital, redemptive relationship to Jesus Christ that a person can have a positive self-esteem.

3) Such a positive self-image is essential to everyone's spiritual and psychological well-being.

4) An unconditional, non-judgmental acceptance by Jesus Christ ought to be announced and proclaimed without differentiating or discriminating to all persons. Both within the church and in evangelistic outreach the gospel must be communicated so as to engender such a positive self-image in those who hear it.

Few evangelical Christians would quarrel with a gospel of self-esteem if understood along the four guidelines listed above. The biblical witness to such a view of self-esteem is clear.

The need for self-esteem as taught by Dr. James Dobson, Dr. Robert Schuller and others has been so stridently denounced by some of their critics that any defense of such a need is seen as a seduction of evangelical Christianity. Some of these critics may be surprised to realize that the above four guidelines were gleaned from Schuller's book *Self-Esteem: The New Reformation* (Word Books, 1982).

This is not to say that Schuller has consistently stayed within his own guidelines in applying his perception of self-esteem. Nevertheless, these expressed guidelines should alert overly zealous critics that they ought not to try to debunk everything that is said about a Christian view of self-esteem.

A Common Need

Schuller's book *Self-Esteem* provides a concept that is desperately needed by the church today. This insight is a gem of truth that came to Schuller as a result of his unflagging effort to bring the gospel to the unchurched. Schuller calls it "God's pathway to human dignity" and expressed it as follows:

What is our Lord's greatest passion for his church today? I believe that he wants his followers to respect themselves as equal children of God and to treat all other human beings with the same respect (*Self-Esteem*, Page 47).

Schuller's insight complements perfectly the perspective formulated by Charles Hodge. A firm biblical basis for Christians "To respect themselves as equal children of God and to treat all other human beings with the same respect," is found in Hodge's observation that "All the descendants of Adam, except those of whom it is expressly revealed that they cannot inherit the kingdom of God, are saved" (Page 3, 4). This is premise B—All persons are elect in Christ except those who the Bible expressly declares will be finally lost.

In his ministry and by his writings Schuller has worked out many of the practical implications of the need for self-esteem. He provides extremely helpful insights regarding the relationship between lack of self-esteem and every form of sin. He has laid the groundwork and given the motivation for the church to work out the implications of the need for self-esteem from a biblical perspective.

Schuller himself is not happy with the term "self-esteem" because it is easily confused with its imitation—sinful pride. As seen in the sin of our first parents, positive self-esteem can be turned into sinful pride. Therefore the biblical guidelines laid out above must be followed in developing a Christian view of self-esteem.

Whether Schuller and others who speak of a Christian self-esteem do so in a consistent and legitimate way can best be determined by applying Schuller's own guidelines to what they say about self-esteem. This is more difficult and more productive than simply denouncing every form of self-esteem.

New Insights

Schuller came to understand the need for self-esteem by discovering the deepest felt need in the hearts of the unchurched people he was trying to reach with the gospel. He found that sinners lack the assurance, comfort, trust and the positive mental attitude that comes from respecting ourselves as children of God. God often provides such insight for understanding an aspect of biblical truth through someone's practical striving to live in obedience to the Word of God. Such an insight may be an authentic instinct.

It was not simply by reading his Bible that Martin Luther received the insight that he could not be made right with God by his deeds. He received this "authentic instinct" by prayerfully striving for many years to be made right with God.

Once Luther received his authentic instinct, the Bible read differently for him and for others with him. Through this process certain truths were set before the church which now appear to be self-evident to us from the pages of Scripture. "For no human being will be justified in his sight by works of the law" (Rom. 3:20).

Testing Our Insights

Although an individual's insight can be a means for discovering truth, the church at large must validate what individuals perceive to be authentic instincts. Our perceived authentic instincts are neither intrinsically trustworthy nor are they to be accepted merely because they are joyfully received by many people. There are two tests for validating such instincts.

There is the consideration of practical application. Theological insights are not useful to God. If they do not help us give greater praise to God and to live more joyfully in his presence we need to have little to do with them.

Schuller's insight passes this test with flying colors. By his ministry Schuller has convincingly demonstrated the desperate need for and the effectiveness of a positive and affirming approach in reaching the unchurched with the gospel. Engendering a positive self-image also helps to provide emotionally and spiritually healthy kingdom workers. Great indeed will be the loss for those denominations and individual Christians who fail to learn from Schuller and others the need for self-esteem and how the gospel fills that need.

Our instincts must be subjected to another test, namely, to examine the Scriptures "to see whether these things be so" (Acts 17:llb). This is essential because God never gives to any one of his Reformers an authentic instinct that comprehends all biblical truth. Our insights must be tested by Scripture to see whether they are of God and to know how they relate to the authentic instincts that God gives to others.

Without biblical validity our perceived authentic instincts rely only on the shifting sands of limited human wisdom. If Self-Esteem Theology is accepted without searching the Scriptures to see whether it is a facet of biblical truth, it will eventually prove to have done more harm than good.

Scripture is the final test. If no biblical basis can be found for Self-Esteem Theology it must be abandoned. To claim, as some do, that all such theologizing is divisive and therefore ought not to be attempted, is to say that we know that our instincts are authentic and whatever God may choose to reveal in his Word about the matter is irrelevant or secondary at best.

Searching for A Biblical Basis

Schuller's insight is that the gospel ought to be communicated, to all persons without differentiating or discriminating in such a way that it will engender a positive self-image in all who hear it. Evangelical Christians ought not to denounce this insight if there is a biblical basis for it.

Schuller's book *Self-Esteem* was his attempt to provide a biblical basis for this insight. He invited others to join him in this venture. The distribution of this book to nearly every religious leader in the United States and Canada proved little and calls into question the notion that for every action there is an equal and opposite reaction. The reaction was opposite, but next to nothing. Few joined him in the venture to find a biblical basis for Self-Esteem Theology, and there is no public evidence that the search continues.

Schuller's attempt to demonstrate a biblical basis for his positive gospel of acceptance and affirmation has been resisted by the evangelical churches. This resistance is not surprising in the light of the history of theology. Nearly all theology is done on the basis of premise A—All persons are outside of Christ (i.e. "lost," "condemned," "on the way to hell," "under law," "children of wrath") except those who the Bible expressly declares will be saved.

This traditional premise cannot provide a biblical warrant for announcing and declaring "good news" to all persons in general or to any person in particular unless there is prior evidence of conversion. Premise A, if consistently applied, provides a basis only for "bad news" coupled with a good suggestion. With the traditional premise, the burden of the church is to tell all nations and every person, that they are lost, condemned, on the way to hell, but if they believe they will be saved (Page 47).

Schuller's positive approach of affirmation and acceptance conflicts with the assumption upon which all evangelical theology has been structured. It is impossible to develop a positive gospel of acceptance and affirmation on the basis of the traditional premise. Any such attempt is bound to fail. Until the church changes its perspective (mind-set) from premise A to premise B (Page 2) it will never find a biblical basis for a gospel of affirmation and acceptance for all who hear.

In his attempt to provide a biblical basis for his positive approach of affirmation and acceptance, Schuller makes claims that evangelical Christians do not, will not, and ought not accept. Among the unacceptable claims Schuller repeatedly makes in his book *Self-Esteem* are the following:

1) By virtue of creation in God's image, every person is a child of God and is worthy of and entitled to recognition from others and a sense of self-esteem. Everyone, he says, has an "estranged Father-child relationship" with God and has infinite value. Even though commonly accepted and very appealing, these concepts are not found in the Scriptures (Chapter Three) and they are in conflict with the guidelines for a biblical doctrine of self-esteem as mentioned above.

On the one hand Schuller correctly acknowledges that it is only by means of an actual, vital, redemptive relationship to Christ that a person can have a positive self-esteem. On the other hand, recognizing the need to address everyone with positive good news, he claims that every person has an "estranged father-child" relationship with God by virtue of their creation in the image of God. Anyone holding firmly to both of these concepts will necessarily be led into Absolute Universalism.

God, the ideal Father with unlimited resources, must necessarily see to it that all the "estranged" relationships with his children are eventually healed (Chapter Three). Absolute Universalism does provide a consistent (but not a biblical) basis for a positive gospel of acceptance and affirmation to all persons.

2) A second claim made by Schuller that cannot stand the test of Scripture is that the *essence* of original sin is "lack of trust." At its core original sin is a weak self-esteem according to Schuller.

Schuller correctly observes that due to Adam's sin everyone is born with a negative self-image that expresses itself in many diverse ways—anxiety, fear, anger, mean rebellion. At a very deep level, he says, sinners are afraid, nontrusting, insecure, self-defensive.

What must be understood, however, is that a corrupted or weak self-image is a *by-product* of sin, not the essence of sin. Just as a positive self-image (recognizing oneself as a child of God for Christ's sake) is a fruit, a *by-product* of salvation, it is not the essence of salvation.

As long as a weak self-image is viewed as the essence of original sin, and a positive self-image is understood to belong to the essence of salvation, no biblical basis will be found for Self-Esteem Theology.

Schuller proclaims his positive gospel of acceptance and affirmation on the basis of what all persons are by reason of their creation in the image of God. He also claims that the sin in which all persons are born is essentially a lack of trust. It is not surprising therefore that many of Schuller's critics accuse him of presenting a hope that is attainable apart from redemption in Christ.

When Schuller appeals to the power of a positive mental attitude, it is not apparent that the appeal is always made within the context of the principles as summarized above. Occasionally Schuller seems to promote a positive mental attitude that is equally as effective for tearing down barns and building bigger ones as it is for seeking first the Kingdom of God.

A Biblical Basis

A biblically warranted assumption is all that we have and all that we need as a basis for a positive ministry of acceptance and affirmation addressed to every person we meet (Chapter Nine). The "universalistic" passages provide the biblical warrant we need for viewing every person we meet as a child of God for whom Christ died, unless we have final and decisive evidence to the contrary. As long as we remain in this life, we will never have such knowledge to the contrary regarding any person or group of persons (Chapter Eight).

The perspective of Biblical Universalism is—All persons are elect in Christ except those who the Bible expressly declares will be finally lost. On this basis all of Christ's followers must "respect themselves as equal children of God and treat all other human beings with the same respect." This basis for a positive ministry of affirmation and acceptance is consistent, as it must be, with the three biblical givens set forth in Chapters Two, Three and Four.

CHAPTER THIRTEEN

Those Who Have Not Heard

IT is conservatively estimated that throughout all of history 75 percent of those who have lived and died have never heard the gospel. Reasonable estimates range as high as 90 percent. Christianity has made little penetration among the established cultures associated with the great world religions—Islam, Hinduism and Buddhism. Statisticians tell us that the balance is not going in favor of Christianity.

Whatever the estimated numbers are, we know that millions of people have lived and died without hearing the gospel. In spite of our best efforts there will be millions more who, through no fault of their own, will live and die without being exposed to the gospel of Jesus Christ in a meaningful way.

Disturbing Questions

Will all those who have not heard the gospel be eternally lost? "There is salvation in no one else, for there is no other name under heaven given among men by which we must be saved" (Acts 4:12). There is an exclusiveness and even a uniqueness about Christianity which may not be compromised in the least degree. "There is one God, and there is one mediator between God and men, the man Christ Jesus" (1 Tim. 2:5).

We may not conclude that God is virtually uninterested in the millions of people who never have the gospel presented to them in a meaningful way. Can it be that God is interested in them but that the fault lies with us and our ancestors who failed to bring the gospel to the unevangelized masses? Our good works do not bring us to salvation. Is the eternal destiny of these millions of people determined by our good works or lack of them?

Many Christians have not dared to ask these kinds of questions ever since they were told that these questions were nothing more than a way of avoiding the decision they had to make in relationship to Jesus Christ. The silence that followed was greatly appreciated by the one to whom these questions were directed. However, intentionally avoiding these questions has often been the occasion for serious inquirers to become skeptical about the claims of the Christian faith.

The question of salvation beyond the reach of the gospel has been made extremely difficult by the fact that all mainstream theology has been done on the basis of premise A—All persons are outside of Christ (i.e. "lost," "condemned," "on the way to hell," "under law," "children of wrath") except those who the Bible expressly declares will be saved.

According to this commonly accepted premise, salvation depends upon sinners fulfilling the condition, requirement, or prescription which is found only in the Bible. From this one must conclude that the unevangelized millions will be finally lost unless they are made aware of the condition or requirement that is *essential* for their salvation.

Proposed Answers

One proposed answer to this problem is that there was sufficient validity in Old Testament revelation for people to experience the grace of God even without a complete New Testament view of Jesus Christ. God also uses the limited validity that is found in non-Christian religions and cultures to place before these people the condition or requirement essential to their salvation.

In neither the Old Testament nor in non-Christian cultures does this validity exist apart from the atoning death of Jesus Christ. Christ's sacrifice is the source of all saving grace. In this way, we are told, both the exclusiveness of Christianity and the possibility of salvation beyond the reach of an explicit New Testament knowledge of Jesus Christ are maintained.

Others say that ever since the coming of Jesus Christ into this world there is no salvation apart from an explicit knowledge of and trust in Jesus Christ as one's Savior and Lord. If no opportunity to believe in Jesus is given during the sinner's earthly so-journ, it must be that at the moment of death or shortly thereafter they will meet Jesus. Everyone must make a personal choice to either accept or reject the grace of God as offered to them in the person of Jesus Christ.

Both of these answers are quite speculative in that there is no direct biblical evidence for them. Furthermore, these answers as well as the answer we will propose in this chapter, raise an obvious objection. The objection is made that if there is salvation beyond the reach of the gospel the motivation or urgency for missionary outreach is diminished. We will address this objection in Chapter Fifteen.

With premise B the salvation of those who have not heard depends neither on a degree of validity in non-Christian religions, nor on a *post mortem* (after death) confrontation with Jesus. In the words of Charles Hodge, "All the descendants of Adam, except those of whom it is expressly revealed that they cannot inherit the kingdom of God, are saved" (Page 3 - 4).

Who "cannot inherit the kingdom of God?" Those, and only those, who in addition to their sin in Adam, throughout their entire life, willfully and finally do not "see fit to acknowledge God" (Rom. 1:28) —whether this refusal is expressed in rebellion against or indifference toward whatever revelation God has given of himself to them (Chapter Four). This perspective allows for the possibility of salvation beyond the reach of the gospel.

Biblical Indications

With premise B we expect to find indications in the Bible that there is salvation beyond the reach of the gospel. Among such indications are these:

1) Those who were saved during Old Testament times did not have an explicit New Testament knowledge of Jesus Christ as their Lord and Savior.

2) No one believes that **all who die in infancy** are excluded from heaven because they fall short of explicit knowledge of the historical Jesus. This implies a salvation beyond the reach of the gospel.

3) There are persons who lived beyond the reach of the Old Testament revelation of God who nevertheless believed in the true

God: Melchizedek (Gen. 14:18, Heb. 7:1); Abimelech (Gen. 20:5); Jethro (Exod. 18:1, 12); Balaam (Num. 22:5, 13); Job (Job 1:1); even Abraham, the father of all believers (Gal. 3:7). The faith that was reckoned to Abraham for righteousness (saving faith), was a faith he had **before** his circumcision (Rom. 4:10, 11). Thus his was neither a New Testament nor an Old Testament faith.

4) "In every nation [including those nations in which the gospel is never preached] any one who fears him and does what is right is acceptable unto him" (Acts 10:34, 35). "When Gentiles who do not have the law do by nature what the law requires, they are a law to themselves, even though they do not have the law. They show that what the law requires is written on their hearts, while their conscience also bears witness and their conflicting thoughts accuse or perhaps excuse them" (Rom. 2:14, 15). "So, if a man who is uncircumcised [lives outside the covenant community of God's people (see Addendum A)] keeps the precepts of the law, will not his uncircumcision be regarded as circumcision?" (Rom. 2:26). "He will justify the circumcised on the ground of their faith and the uncircumcised through their faith" (Rom. 3:30).

5) The men of Athens were worshipping the God Paul had not yet proclaimed to them: "What therefore you worship as unknown, this I proclaim to you" (Acts 17:23).

6) "For every one who does evil hates the light [Jesus and his gospel] and does not come to the light [does not embrace the gospel] lest his deeds should be exposed. But he who does what is true comes to the light [embraces the gospel when it is presented to him or her] that it may be clearly seen that his deeds have been wrought in God" (John 3:19-21). Some come to the light not that their works may be of God, but "that it may be clearly seen" that their works were wrought in God.

7) We can also look to the parable of the last judgment (Matt. 25:31-46). Without **imposed restrictions,** this passage appears to teach that every person's eternal destiny is determined by the good works they do, or fail to do, in this present life.

One way **to restrict** the application of this parable is to claim that "the least" (those benefited by the works being judged), refers to disciples, those who were "prophets." Appeal is made to Matt. 10:42 which refers to the hospitality that would be shown to "these little ones" (presumably the missionaries sent out by Jesus).

However, the context of Matthew 10:42 speaks not only of those who receive a "prophet," but also those who receive "a righteous man," that is, one who practices true religion. This extends the beneficiaries far beyond missionaries, especially in the light of indication number 4 (above).

Another way the application of this passage is restricted is by saying that "my brethren" (Matt. 25:40) is a very limited reference. Matthew, we are told, consistently limits the concept of "brethren" to the twelve apostles or perhaps to professing Christians.

But in Matthew 12:50 Jesus explains: "For whoever does the will of my Father in heaven is my brother . . ." In the light of indication number 4 (above), there is no limit to those who may represent Christ to us as we provide for their needs. It is this judgment scene itself that describes for us who were doing "the will of my Father" and thus practicing true religion.

According to this parable of the sheep and the goats, we ought to assume that everyone who hungers or has other needs represents Christ as the beneficiary of our good deeds. This is consistent with the premise that we ought to view all persons as members of the body of Christ unless we have decisive and final evidence to conclude otherwise. Whatever we do for the benefit of others Jesus Christ will consider it as having been done unto him.

The language used in this parable of the judgment scene does not allow any limitation or restriction as it describes the final judgment. "Before him will be gathered all the nations, and he will separate them one from another as a shepherd separates the sheep from the goats" (Matt. 25:32). Some of these nations were never visited by an evangelist, disciple, or a professing Christian. Nevertheless Matthew 25:31-46 reveals the basis upon which the inhabitants of "all the nations" will be judged.

In his enlightening little book *Work The Meaning of Your Life*, (Christian's Library Press, P. O. Box 2226, Grand Rapids, MI 49501), Dr. Lester DeKoster expounds on the scene depicted in Matt 25:31-46. He makes the very significant point that the service done for others cannot be some occasional, incidental or part time activity. Why not? The evaluation of that service determines eternal destiny. This cannot be an activity that is incidental to, or only a small part of, the person's entire life. The deeds that were done or left undone reflect the basic attitude and pattern of that person's life commitment.

This parable of the Final Judgment addresses the fact that human beings have many needs. DeKoster correctly understands that what Jesus is saying is that "where humans are hungry, there He [Christ] chooses to hunger." In broad terms Jesus is speaking about all the physical, emotional, social, and spiritual needs that human beings have.

The needs of mankind are not met by an occasional gesture of goodwill and hospitality on the part of a handful of people. The needs of human beings are met by those who labor in all the various occupations, industries, businesses and professions every day of their life. It is our daily work that takes up by far the largest proportion of our alloted number of wakeful hours and gives meaning to our lives.

DeKoster defines our daily work as "The opportunity God gives us to make ourselves useful to others." It is basically in and through our daily work that the needs of mankind are met, as those needs are depicted in broad outline in this parable of the Last Judgment. God chooses to be served through our regular daily work and other deeds in which we are helpful to others. Therefore "Whatever your task, work heartily, as serving the Lord and not men, knowing that from the Lord you will receive the inheritance as your reward; you are serving the Lord Christ" (Col. 3:23, 24).

Throughout our lifetime we either serve ourselves or some creaturely goal in our daily work and in our other activities, thereby shaping ourselves as goats; or, we spend our time and energies serving God in the way in which we make ourselves useful to others. Those who so serve others are the sheep. The day of judgment *will not make* those who are to be judged into sheep or goats. The judgment day will publicly display and disclose *those who are* goats and separate them from the sheep.

This parable of the last judgment has the broadest application possible. It reveals the standard by which all persons will be judged on the last day. The final separation on the day of judgment will not take place on the basis of an explicit knowledge of and faith in the New Testament view of Jesus Christ. Whether they lived in the spirit of kindness and mercy, spending time, energy and possessions to be of service to others in their need is the standard by which all persons shall be judged. Such deeds can be done, or left undone, by either those who have heard the gospel or by those who live their entire life beyond the reach of the gospel.

This understanding of the parable of the Last Judgment is not moralism, that is, salvation by good works. The good deeds that will meet God's approval on the day of judgment are not works that earn or merit God's favor and our salvation. There is only one basis for salvation and that forever remains the sovereign electing grace of God in Jesus Christ our Lord.

What this passage teaches us is that the good deeds done by the children of men are **the evidence** that these "sheep" lived by the Spirit of Christ that was working in them. "What the law requires [was] written on their hearts" (Rom 2:15). "What does the Lord require of you but to do justice, to love mercy and to talk humbly with your God?" (Micah 6:8). True religion is: "To visit orphans and widows in their affliction, and to keep oneself unstained from the world" (James 1:27).

No one can so live except the Spirit of Christ be in him or her. The "goats" are revealed to be "goats" because they refused to walk in obedience to the will of God as it had been made known to them.

"According to What A Man Has"

We noticed in Chapter Ten that, in the very nature of the case, all the demands to repent, believe and to live in obedience to God's will as revealed in the Bible come only to responsible persons who are meaningfully confronted with the promise and demands of the gospel. For such persons faith is absolutely necessary and unbelief is damnable. This is so not because such faith is the one prerequisite or condition without which God is either unable or unwilling to save sinners. Such repentance, faith, and obedience is absolutely necessary for those to whom the gospel is proclaimed because any other response is a refusal to do what God has revealed as his will for these people.

We have no right, however, to take what is required of those who have the gospel proclaimed to them and conclude that the identical demands are made of every person everywhere whether they ever hear the gospel or not. "If the readiness is there, it is acceptable according to what a man has, not according to what he has not" (2 Cor. 8:12). This is the biblical, obviously just and gracious criteria which Paul applies to the matter of giving to those who are in need.

This same standard is reflected in Acts 10:35: "God shows no partiality, but in every nation any one who fears him and does what is right is acceptable to him." The standard by which all will be judged on that final day is piety toward God and doing what is right, according to the light and privileges which that person had received.

Because God is a law unto himself, we cannot question the fact that he is able to save whom he will even among those who have never heard the gospel. He has chosen to save all persons except those, and only those, who, in addition to their sin in Adam, willfully and finally refuse to acknowledge God—whether this refusal is expressed in rebellion against or indifference to whatever revelation God has given of himself to them (Chapter Four). We must, therefore, allow for the possibility that some who live their entire life beyond the reach of the gospel may be saved by God's grace given to them in Jesus Christ our Lord.

CHAPTER FOURTEEN

Thinking Further

A) Are There Few That Will be Saved?

The premise—All persons are elect in Christ except those who the Bible expressly declares will be finally lost—raises certain questions. We wish to consider some of the questions that come to mind in connection with the perspective of Biblical Universalism.

The traditional view—All persons are outside of Christ except those who the Bible expressly declares will be saved—seems to imply that most persons will be finally lost. The perspective we are considering seems to imply that most persons will be saved.

Nothing is gained by speculating about "few" or "many." Jesus himself refused to be drawn into a discussion about this question when he was specifically asked the question "Lord, will those who are saved be few?" (Luke 13:23). The Bible does not provide an answer to this question. Neither the traditional perspective nor the premise I am advocating addresses the question of whether few or many will be saved.

It might be best to drop the discussion at this point. However, there is a general impression that the Bible seems to indicate that proportionally "few" will be saved. I would like to consider why we have such an impression. I do so not in order to argue the opposite point of view, namely, that most people will be saved, but rather to point out that we ought not to draw a conclusion one way or the other on the basis of the assumption with which we work.

Scarcity Increases Value—Most things are increased or decreased in value depending on how plentiful or scarce they may be. An illustration of this is the value that has been placed upon such a commodity as salt. There was a time when salt was so scarce that it was used as money. Although the chemical composition of salt has not changed it has become so plentiful that it can no longer serve as a medium of exchange.

The value we place on almost everything is in inverse proportion to its availability. If diamonds were as plentiful as gravel there would be times when we would pay someone to haul them away from our property.

Salvation is one thing that is not in the least bit diminished in value no matter how readily available and great its supply. It is offered unconditionally to one and all. The price is right: "Come, buy wine and milk without money and without price" (Isa. 55:1). The assurance is given: "For everyone who asks receives, and he who seeks finds, and to him who knocks it will be opened" (Matt. 7:8). The command is "Go out to the highways and hedges, and compel people to come in, that my house may be filled" (Luke 14:23). The invitation we hear is "The Spirit and the Bride say, 'Come.' And let him who hears say, 'Come.' and let him who is thirsty come, let him who desires take the water of life without price" (Rev. 22:17).

What cannot be said about salvation is that it is scarce, that few are able to find it, or that when found it is attained only by way of a difficult struggle and great effort. The banquet hall is large and the provisions are ample, and the people should be compelled to come in. Salvation is not difficult to find. In fact, everyone who seeks it finds it. Rather than being difficult to attain, it is freely given by sheer grace. "Where sin increased, grace abounded all the more" (Rom. 5:20). The number of those who attain it is "a great multitude which no man could number, from every nation, from all tribes and peoples and tongues" (Rev. 7:9).

Kingdom Parables—However, in order to express the extremely high value of salvation, the kingdom parables picture salvation as something that is rare, difficult to find or hard to attain. Each parable has a specific lesson and none of them is intended to satisfy our curiosity about the relative number of those who will be saved or finally lost. The extremely high value of the kingdom of heaven is revealed in these words of Jesus:

> The kingdom of heaven is like a treasure hidden in a field, which a man found and covered up; then in his joy he

goes and sells all that he has and buys the field. Again, the kingdom of heaven is like a merchant in search of fine pearls, who, on finding one pearl of great value, went and sold all that he had and bought it (Matt. 13:44, 45).

What we said about the value of diamonds if they were as plentiful as gravel applies equally well to hidden treasures and outstandingly beautiful pearls. The parables of the Hidden Treasure and Pearl of Great Price teach us that we should seek first of all the kingdom of heaven and every other consideration ought to be secondary to this purpose. These parables do **not intend** to tell us that very rarely is someone fortunate enough to find the kingdom of heaven.

So also the words of Jesus, "For the gate is narrow and the way is hard, that leads to life, and those who find it are few" (Matt. 7:14) should not be understood to say that the way of salvation is hard to find, that after finding it is difficult to attain, with the result that few will be saved. As a matter of fact, Matthew 7:8 tells us quite the opposite—every one who asks receives, all those who seek find, and to all those who knock it is opened.

The "narrow gate," "hard way," and "few finding" convey the thought of the intrinsic value of salvation, not the extent of its availability. These expressions have the same meaning as finding a "hidden treasure" or "a pearl of great price." The lesson of "narrow gate," "the hard way," and "few finding" is: covet salvation as a rare discovery, an invaluable treasure; be willing to forsake all other interests in order to attain its desired end; it is worth every effort necessary to find it. An attitude of thoughtlessly drifting along with the crowd is a sure sign that one is not on the road that leads to glory.

Neither Matthew 7:8 with its apparent unlimited access, nor Matthew 7:14 with its seeming restricted access, is a numerical calculation regarding the relative number of persons who will be saved or finally lost. The observation has been correctly made that there is no more reason to conclude from the parable of the Two Ways that few will be saved, than there is to conclude from the parable of the Ten Virgins (Matt. 25:1-13) that precisely as many will be saved as will be finally lost.

Few Are Chosen—We must also consider Matthew 22:l4, "For many are called, but few are chosen." The first thing we must recognize is that this verse is a conclusion drawn at the end of a series of parables in which Jesus was talking about the chief priests and the Pharisees—"When the chief priests and the Pharisees heard his parables, they perceived that he was speaking about them" (Matt. 21:45).

The entire series of parables (beginning at Matt. 21:33) has reference to the historical fact that the religious leaders and most of the God's covenant people did not respond favorably to Jesus' earthly ministry. "He came to his own home, and his own people received him not" (John 1:11). Therefore the gospel call would be extended to the ends of the earth. We see this historical development come to expression in the ministry of Paul and Barnabas: "It was necessary that the Word of God should be spoken first to you. Since you thrust it from you, and judge yourselves unworthy of eternal life, behold, we turn to the Gentiles" (Acts 13:46).

In saying "Many are called but few are chosen," Jesus was talking about the fact that during his own ministry he called many and few responded. This is the theme found in the entire series of parables. In Matthew 21:33-41 we find the parable of the wicked caretakers who plotted to kill the son of the of the householder. Jesus spoke about the "stone which the builders rejected" in Matthew 21:42, 43. These obviously are references to the kind of reception Jesus received from his countrymen. This same theme of Jesus being rejected by his own people is continued in Matthew 22.

In the parable of the Wedding Feast (Matt. 22:1-14), Jesus is the son for whom the marriage feast had been prepared. Those who were first invited and expected to attend "made light" of the invitation. The invitation then went out to those in "the thoroughfares" with the intention and the result "that the wedding hall was *filled with guests*" (vs. 10, Emphasis Added).

Although one guest was not properly dressed and was therefore cast out, one thing this parable **does not** teach is that God's plan of salvation concludes with "few" attending the wedding feast of his son. "Many are called, but few are chosen" refers to the fact that few of his countrymen responded to Jesus' invitation and therefore **many** from among the Gentiles were invited and came.

B) Not For is Against

Jesus said "He who is not with me is against me, and he who does not gather with me scatters" (Matt. 12:30). This appears to be the very opposite of the premise we propose in this study. It seems to say that we should assume that those who have not given evidence of being "with" Jesus are against him.

The statement is a strong reminder that in the great battle between Christ and Satan no one can remain neutral. There are only two kingdoms. The kingdom of God, with Christ as its head, and the kingdom of Satan. Those who do not seek to gather together those who belong to Christ are willing to leave them to become the prey of Satan. Neutrality is impossible.

The fact that there is no neutrality in the struggle between the kingdom of light and the kingdom of darkness can be, and is, stated conversely depending on the circumstances—"He that is not against us is for us" (Mark 9:40); or, "He that is not against you is for you" (Luke 9:50). In either case these declarations neither support nor refute the premise we seek to establish in this study.

C) Assurance of Salvation

We can have full assurance of salvation only when we come to know and believe that salvation is entirely the work of God. To insert any human act or attitude as *essential* to our salvation is to subject the believer to perpetual uncertainty. To base our assurance of salvation on anything other than, or in addition to, God's completed work in Christ leads to uncertainty and distrust.

We are not saved by anything we do—not even by our "decision" to believe. The "decision" to believe is evidence of our salvation, it is not a condition or requisite for being accepted by God (See Chapter Ten). Scripture says: "It depends not upon man's will or exertion, but upon God's mercy" (Rom. 9:16). Our faith is a fruit of our union with Christ. By the time a person is so changed that he is willing to accept grace he is no longer the old man, the natural man, who regards the gospel as foolishness. Such a person has a new heart that has learned to recognize the "good news" as the wisdom that comes from God.

The personal act of faith is never flawless. How grateful every Christian should be that their salvation does not depend on his or her faith. There are many sincere Christians, who, neither rejecting nor remaining indifferent to the promises and claims of Christ in the gospel, find it difficult to come to assurance of salvation. They view the gospel as a conditional promise and not as unconditional good news. Consequently they are plagued by doubts: "Do I love him enough?" "Is my faith strong enough?" "If you only knew how sinful I am!" "Have I truly repented?" "Am I fully committed to Christ?" "Will I remain faithful to the end?"

Satan tempts us to think that we must *do something* in order to be saved. Every religious tradition (pagan and Christian) has its program of "works." If nothing else you must repent or you must believe in order to be saved.

On the one hand, such a conditional salvation leads to spiritual pride in those who think they have fulfilled the required condition. On the other hand, among those who correctly sense that they do not have the power within themselves to meet the condition, this inability is looked upon as evidence that there is no "good news" for them.

Although not so intended, it is cruel to say to those who have difficulty coming to assurance of salvation: "Well, you believe don't you?" It is that very act of faith, or the strength of that faith, that they are questioning. It is no comfort whatever then to tell them that their salvation depends on their faith.

There is biblical warrant for believing that all persons are elect in Christ except those who, in addition to their sin in Adam, personally, willfully and finally remain indifferent or reject the knowledge of God that has been given to them. Those lacking in assurance must be encouraged to trust the biblical witness that "he gave himself a ransom for all," except only those who willfully and finally choose to "refuse to have God in their knowledge."

The response of Biblical Universalism to all those who sincerely inquire about the assurance of their salvation is this: "The gospel is meant for you unless you are indifferent toward it or willfully reject it." They may be assured that no sin or weakness (including the weakness of faith) that remains in them against their will can hinder them from being received of God in grace and being worthy partakers of the cup of salvation.

CHAPTER FIFTEEN

Motives for Missions

THROUGHOUT this study we have been contending that the over-all message of Scripture is that—All persons are elect in Christ except those who the Bible expressly declares will be finally lost. Those who will be finally lost are described in the Bible in no other way than as those, and only those who, in addition to their sin in Adam, decisively and finally do not see fit "to acknowledge God" according to whatever revelation God has given of himself to them (Chapter Four). This premise allows the possibility that some persons, who live their entire life beyond the reach of the gospel may be saved (See Chapter Thirteen).

An objection to this premise of Biblical Universalism has been raised not by missionaries themselves so much as by missiologists (those who study the theory of missions). The objection is that if there is the possibility of persons being saved without the gospel reaching them during their lifetime, the primary motivation for world missionary enterprise, namely, to save persons from eternal condemnation, is lost. Why send missionaries if those living in non-Christian lands can be saved without these sacrificial endeavors? This objection deserves a response.

Preliminary Considerations

The question is not whether God has the right to leave these vast numbers of persons to suffer the just consequences of their sin. He undoubtedly has the sovereign right to do so. The question is whether God is able and willing to save anyone from among those

93

who have lived and died without being exposed to the gospel in a meaningful way.

To conclude that God is not interested in the salvation of the millions of persons who never hear the gospel does violence to the revelation that God has given of himself in Christ Jesus. Therefore some thoughtful Christians have begun to consider the possibility that these unevangelized people will be confronted by Jesus Christ at the moment of death or shortly thereafter. At that time they will have the opportunity to make their decision either for or against Jesus Christ.

Besides having little direct biblical evidence in favor of it, this *post mortem* (after death) theory faces the same objection that is registered against Biblical Universalism. It allows the possibility of salvation apart from hearing the gospel during one's earthly life. The fact that such a theory is proposed indicates that there is the felt need among evangelical Christians for re-thinking the issue of motivation for world missions.

Neither Biblical Universalism nor any other view may be judged unacceptable simply because we suspect it may detract from the urgency for the world mission enterprise. If there is scriptural warrant for the premise of Biblical Universalism, we must adjust our thinking to it whether in our opinion it will stimulate mission outreach or not.

Before consideration of any other motivation for mission outreach we must realize that above all else we have the command of Christ: "Go therefore and make disciples of all nations" (Matt. 28:19). Keeping this thought in mind we can consider further response to the stated objection.

There are not two gospels, one for church people and another for the unchurched or unreached. Neither are there two different bases for announcing and declaring the good news together with the command to repent and believe. (See Chapter Eight.) Whatever motivation there is for propagating the gospel from one generation to the next within the covenant community of God's people (See Addendum A.) applies equally well for proclaiming the gospel to all persons in every nation. This motivation evolves from both a consideration of what may follow if one does not communicate the gospel and from the blessedness that derives from proclaiming the good news.

All Mentally Competent Persons Have a Choice to Make

What may follow if the church does not proclaim the gospel? Biblical Universalism takes with utmost seriousness the real significance of the human decision to reject or ignore the revelation God gives of himself in either creation/conscience or gospel proclamation. There is a decisive power in the human choice to refuse "to acknowledge God" (Rom. 1:28). Such refusal sets in motion a hardening process which, if persisted in, ends in eternal death.

Although this goes beyond our ability to understand, sinners do have within themselves the ability to persist in unbelief, indifference and disobedience, thereby bringing eternal and fatal consequences upon themselves (See Chapter Seven.). Every person, apart from the renewing electing grace of God, continues to follow a self-chosen path of exchanging "the truth about God for a lie" (Rom. 1:25). It is **possible** that everyone living beyond the reach of the gospel continues to reject whatever revelation God gives of himself to him or her.

Biblical Universalism underscores the fact that, if such is the case, the lostness of each of these persons is not due to God's indifference or to the fact that the gospel did not reach them. Their eternal condemnation will be wholly attributable to the fact that they willfully and finally rejected whatever revelation of God's will had been given to them.

This, however, is not the power of contrary choice. That is, sinners are not in a neutral position from which they can choose good or evil. By reason of the universal enslavement to sin, no one conceived and born in sin has the capacity within himself or herself to choose the good. No sinner can sovereignly decide to believe. "Without me you can do nothing" (John 15:5). "No one can come to me unless the Father who sent me draws him" (John 6:44).

There is only one means that God has **revealed** to us and made available for use by the church to turn the hearts of sinners away from the pathway of self-destruction. The church has been commanded to use that means: "Go therefore and make disciples of all nations, baptizing them in the name of the Father and of the Son and of the Holy Spirit, teaching them to observe all that I have commanded you" (Matt. 28:19, 20).

Because no other means has been **revealed** to us whereby sinners can come to active, comforting, joyful fellowship with God, Paul has good reason to appeal to our conscience by asking "How are men to call upon him in whom they have not believed? And how are they to believe in him whom they have not heard? And how are they to hear without a preacher?" (Rom. 10:14).

No other means has been entrusted to the church to move sinners to repentance, faith and grateful obedience, than the proclamation of the gospel of peace. Nowhere can sinners see the ugliness of their sin and the astonishing light of God's redeeming love as clearly as in "Jesus Christ and him crucified" (1 Cor. 2:2).

The fact that God has not revealed any other means to us is not to say that God is unable or unwilling to use some means **not revealed** to us, to create new life in those who by nature are dead in sin. The Bible simply does not speak directly to this question.

Christian parents, even though they have biblical warrant for viewing their children as children of God, must use the biblically revealed means of grace, trusting that God will be pleased to use the Word and sacraments to create faith in the hearts of their children. They recognize the awesome reality that their children might not walk in God's appointed way, and that by their unbelief and willful disobedience they could bring God's final judgment upon themselves. Therefore these parents prayerfully and diligently lead their children in the way of salvation by nurturing them in the truth of what God in Christ has done for them.

So also Biblical Universalism recognizes the dreadful reality that those living beyond the reach of the gospel are able, and by nature are inclined, to "refuse to have God in their knowledge." Therefore, with life or death urgency, the church must go to make disciples of them, teaching them to observe all that Christ has commanded us (Matt. 28:19, 20). We are conscience bound to diligently and intently use the means given to the church so that all persons everywhere may hear "the very words of God" (Rom. 3:2, NIV).

This must be done so that those living outside of the church will not harden themselves in the service of sin. The "very words of God" consist of the good news of what God in Christ has done for us, together with the command to repent and believe the gospel.

We see a parallel of the "real significance" of the human decision in the context of unconditional good news in Acts 27:21 through 32. Paul announced, declared, the unconditional good news, "I now bid you take heart; for there will be no loss of life among you, but only of the ship" (vs. 22). Nevertheless the consequences would have been fatal if the passengers did not heed the warning that came later—"Unless these men stay in the ship, you cannot be saved" (vs. 31). There is a triumph of grace in Christ Jesus which is to be **announced and declared** to all people, and all persons share in this victory *except those* who stubbornly and finally "suppress the truth" (Rom. 1:18) and do "not see fit to acknowledge God" (Rom. 1:28).

The Joy and Blessing That Come Through Gospel Proclamation

What advantage, purpose or motivation is there for bringing the gospel to all persons everywhere if it is possible for God to save his people without their being exposed to the New Testament view of Christ during their earthly life? This in essence is the question asked in Romans 3:1, "Then what advantage has the Jew? Or what is the value of Circumcision?"

This question can be legitimately asked as follows: "What advantage does the member of God's covenant community of people (the church member) have? What is the value of baptism?" (See page 116.) If there is the possibility of salvation beyond the reach of the gospel, why try to incorporate those persons living in non-Christian lands into the fellowship of the visible church?

Paul does not say that the advantage of being part of the covenant people of God (a church member) is that among them, and **only among them,** there is salvation. The advantage of being incorporated into the covenant community of God's people is "Much in every way. To begin with [they] are entrusted with the very words of God" (Rom. 3:2 NIV). The reference is to the Old Testament as the "very words of God." How much greater is the advantage to those who are incorporated into the community of God's people today! They have been entrusted with both the Old and the New Testament special revelation of God. The sign or seal of God's commitment and promise of grace has been given to them.

What fellowship, joy, light, comfort, hope, vision, encouragement, peace, nurturing, wisdom is ours because we are part of the community of believers to whom "the very words of God" have been entrusted and to whom God has explicitly declared his attitude of grace and sealed his commitment of favor with the sign of baptism! (See Addendum A.) Even if we were given to know that all those living in non-Christian lands were certain to be saved without hearing the gospel, what a delight and joy it would be to bring the "good news" of what God in Christ has done **for us.**

When we view all other human beings as fellow heirs of the kingdom of heaven, we become eager to share with them the joy and the hope that is ours in Christ, while in the spirit of love we warn them against unbelief and sin. "Out of the abundance of the heart the mouth speaks" (Matt. 12:34b).

Although we view those living in non-Christian lands as God's elect, we know that they have not yet come to a saving knowledge of Jesus Christ. We know that they are ill-equipped to glorify God and to enjoy him forever, which is the chief purpose of man. "Without God's special redemptive disclosure ["the very words of God"], his will for our being and conduct in each and every area of life remains in a significant sense 'unknown'" (Dr. Henry Stob, *Calvin Theological Journal*, April 1985, p. 65).

We can benefit from an extension of the analogy given by Dr. John Murray: "To say to the slave who has not been emancipated 'Do not behave as a slave' is to mock his enslavement. But to say the same to the slave who has been set free is the necessary appeal to put into effect the privileges and rights of his liberation" (page 51).

What is this but to say that in approaching those who by nature are bondservants of sin we must assume that they have been set free in Christ? To say to those for whom we have no warrant for assuming they have been emancipated "Do not behave as a slave" is to mock their enslavement.

> Just as President Lincoln signed the Emancipation Proclamation and, by the stroke of a pen, objectively freed every Black American slave, so Jesus Christ, by his obedience in life and unto death, objectively saved every human being who finally will be saved. And just as no American slave personally enjoyed the benefits of Lincoln's act until he or she heard and believed the good news of emancipation, so no redeemed sinner subjectively enjoys Christ's redemption now except through the preaching and belief of the

gospel. In this sense, we are being saved even now (I Cor. 1:18; Acts 16:31; Rom. 10:9).

Until men and women learn of the good news of their salvation, they continue to live as if nothing had happened. They remain as they had been—without hope, not knowing God, unaware of his forgiveness and favor. The gospel ministry is for the sake of such men and women—that they may obtain salvation, subjectively as well as objectively. "Therefore I endure everything for the sake of the elect, that they may obtain salvation in Christ with its eternal glory" (2 Tim. 2:10). (See Edward Fudge, Addendum B, page 125.)

To view those to whom we bring the gospel as those who are elect in Christ does not decrease mission motivation. It is this perspective that is the divinely revealed motive for going forth with the gospel. "Do not be afraid, but speak and do not be silent . . . for I have many people in this city" (Acts 18: 9, 10).

The Word of God must go forth into all the world "that the man of God may be complete, equipped for every good work" (2 Tim. 3:17). God wants all of his people to be equipped "for the work of ministry, for building up the body of Christ, until we all attain to the unity of faith and of the knowledge of the Son of God, to mature manhood, to the measure of the stature of the fullness of Christ" (Eph. 4:13).

What advantage is there in gathering all of God's people into the visible church? "Much in every way! First of all, they have been entrusted with the very words of God" (Rom. 3:2, NIV).

CHAPTER SIXTEEN

The Message of Missions

THE gospel is preached so that those who hear may repent and believe. "[Jesus] came into Galilee, preaching the gospel of God, and saying, 'The time is fulfilled, and the kingdom of God is at hand; repent, and believe in the gospel'" (Mark 1:l4, 15). After his ascension, the apostles came "testifying both to Jews and to Greeks of repentance to God and faith in our Lord Jesus Christ" (Acts 20:21).

The need for forgiveness must be felt before there can be any appreciation for the announcement of forgiveness. From this fact the erroneous conclusion is sometimes drawn that the message of missions is first of all a declaration of God's wrath in order to make the sinner responsive to God's love. Sinners, it is thought, must *acknowledge* and perhaps even confess their sin in order to be willing to receive God's grace.

"The Wrath of God is Revealed"

The thought that the message of missions is first of all a message of wrath, in order to get the sinners to recognize the need of forgiving grace, assumes that those sinners are not aware of God's wrath. Such is not the case. God has already spoken to all persons about his wrath. "For the wrath of God is revealed from heaven against all ungodliness and wickedness of men who by their wickedness suppress the truth" (Rom. 1:8).

There are many searching souls whose thoughts "accuse them" and whose "conscience also bears witness" against them (Rom. 2:15). They are deeply troubled because they know they have

101

provoked the just anger of an invisible and awesome power. The
extremes to which many go in sacrificing their possessions, their
bodies, and even their own children, in order to appease the "gods"
whom they consider to be against them testifies to the seriousness
with which they view their plight.

Although civilized people express these anxieties in different,
subtle, and often unrecognized ways, they demonstrate that what
God's law requires is written on their hearts, and that their consciences accuse them. "O that we might see some good!" (Ps. 4:6)
is the plaintive cry of all except those who have stubbornly hardened
themselves in sin. Henry David Thoreau was right: "The mass of
men live lives of quiet desperation."

Why desperation? God's general revelation informs them that
they are without excuse! Their consciences accuse them and so
they try by every means possible to cover their sin and not even
admit the reality of that sin to themselves. Self-preservation demands that they deny the existence of sin within themselves. They
are afraid, nontrusting, insecure, self-defensive. This expresses
itself at times as anger and mean rebellion. They live in fear no
matter how they try to mask that fear. What they need to know is
that the same holiness which accuses them has provided a full and
free forgiveness for their sins.

The Good News of Grace

There are occasions when sinners must hear of the reality of
judgment in order that they may sense the need to repent and to
turn to Christ as their only refuge. Wrath and judgment, however,
ought not to be the first word for those who have not heard the
good news. God's grace is the loud accent of the message of
Scripture, and God's wrath is revealed so that sinners will not think
lightly of rejecting God's promise of grace. "God's kindness is
meant to lead you to repentance" (Rom. 2:4).

It is only when they are assured of an unconditional acceptance
by God that they dare to admit to themselves, to God, and to others
that they are sinners worthy of judgment. Therefore John Calvin
says "We mean to show that a man cannot apply himself seriously
to repentance without knowing himself to belong to God. But no
one is truly persuaded he belongs to God unless he has **first**

recognized God's grace" (*Calvin's Institutes*, III, iii, 2 emphasis added).

There is a correlation between repentance and God's grace. They cannot exist separately. They are not, however, mutually dependent. Grace has a priority! Repentance may not be presented as a condition or requirement which moves God to extend grace to sinners. Repentance itself is a gift from God and it is part of the grace of God. Jesus Christ was raised from the dead in order "to give repentance to Israel and forgiveness of sins" (Acts 5:31). This same gift is given to the Gentiles: "Then to the Gentiles also God has granted repentance unto life" (Acts ll:18).

To be Announced and Declared to All

The required response to the gospel (the good news) must not be presented as though it is prescription, condition or requirement which will move God to grant us his salvation. Consider this conversation between a non-Christian interpreter and a missionary. After reading Luke 23, the interpreter asked "Why had Jesus to suffer all this?" The missionary replied: "He gave His life for you and me." "For me also?" "Yes, also for you," replied the missionary, "if you believe in Him."

One wonders why the missionary's answer to the second question was not simply "Yes, for you also," since he had already told the interpreter that Christ had given his life for him. The answer that was given is so familiar it seems appropriate. Is this truly the teaching of God's Word, "Yes, he died for you, if you do something"? Good news cannot be presented conditionally (See Chapter Nine.). How much more comforting and challenging it would be to say "Yes, for you also, and therefore you must believe in him."

Many extended answers could be given. None of them should be presented as a condition or requirement for salvation but as an announcement of good news which requires an appropriate response. "Yes, for you also, and therefore you must repent" (Mark l:14). "Yes, for you also and therefore you must deny yourself, take up your cross and follow him" (Matt. 16:24). "Yes, for you also and therefore you must consider yourself dead to sin and alive to God" (Rom. 6:ll). "Yes, for you also and therefore you must not walk after the flesh but after the Spirit" (Rom. 8:4) and so on.

The purpose of gospel proclamation is not to explain the terms by which sinners can induce God to save them. No act or attitude of repentance, faith or obedience can be *essential* in establishing us in the state of grace. Any human act, even though directed by the Holy Spirit, insofar as it remains the sinner's act or attitude, is tainted with sin and is as imperfect as a "polluted garment" (Isa. 64:6). Nothing imperfect or stained with sin can be *essential* to salvation.

Repentance, like faith, is absolutely necessary for all those who hear the gospel. But not because repentance is a condition, requirement or prescription for the miracle of grace to occur. Those who hear the good news and refuse to repent thereby reject the will of God as it is made known to them. Such willful and final indifference or rejection of God's revealed will becomes the just cause for their condemnation (Chapter Ten).

Peace Between God and Man

Jesus Christ was sent to "preach good news," "proclaim release," (Luke 4:18). Paul says of Christ, "He came and preached peace to you who were far off and peace to those who were near" (Eph. 2:17), referring to both those who were members of the covenant community and to those who were outside the community of God's people.

An attitude of favor and grace is revealed to the woman and her seed in Genesis 3:15. There would be "enmity between" the seed of the woman and the seed of the serpent. By implication the seed of the woman would be friends of God. That favor and grace is merited by the "bruising" of Christ and is enjoyed by all the descendants of Adam and Eve except those who willfully turn from the goodness of God.

The absence of peace and the resulting sword of which Jesus spoke in Matthew 10:34 is not an allusion to a division between God and those to whom the good news would come. The reference is to the hostility which would ensue between those who accept and those who reject the message of peace. The message itself, to all "who are far off and to those who are near," consists of the publication of peace between God and man.

This proclamation of peace can be announced and declared to all persons without differentiating or discriminating only on the assumption that—All persons are elect in Christ (that is "will be saved," "justified," "on the way to heaven," "under grace," "children of God") except those who the Bible expressly declares will be finally lost. On the basis of this assumption we may tell all people what God has done for them in his Son! The awesome truth about God's wrath is to be reserved for those who remain indifferent to or reject this good news which the church has been commissioned to proclaim to *all people*.

Those who pray and work for a response of repentance, faith and obedience in those they approach with the gospel must view those persons as elect in Christ. Saving faith is a personal belief on the part of a particular sinner that not only others but also that he or she has been forgiven and has been made right with God. If the Bible does not (and therefore we may not) tell sinners that their sins have been forgiven, on what testimony or witness are they to base their belief that their sins have been forgiven?

What God Has Done for Us

We must identify ourselves with those to whom we bring the gospel, respecting them as equally children of God together with us, looking upon them as those who belong to Christ and for whom Christ died.

Premise B is the biblically warranted assumption, perspective, mind-set, from which we may view those to whom we bring the gospel. The question of how, when, and even if we are to make this assumption known to the persons we approach with the gospel must be answered according to particular circumstances, with enlightened Christian discernment seeking the guidance of the Holy Spirit.

This perspective does not prevent us from issuing a most earnest and clear call for repentance to those who are living in open, blatant, defiant unbelief and sin. They may need nothing so much as to be strongly and repeatedly warned that they must repent of their sin, and be told that if continue as they are they will surely bring upon themselves God's final expression of wrath.

Such a warning is fully consistent with the assumption that they are elect children of God. Our hope and trust is that God will be pleased to use our strong warning to make them see the seriousness of their sin, repent of it, and turn to the pathway of trust and joyful obedience. This perspective will keep us from a spirit of vindictiveness.

An aged widowed saint had an alcoholic son with whom she lived and for whom she prayed every day for 45 years. She repeatedly told me (long after I, as a practical matter, could any longer so view him), "I believe he is a child of God who is walking on the wrong path." Yet, how lovingly and forcefully with full conviction she told him time and again: "Ralph (a fictitious name), if you continue to get drunk, you will go to hell, because the Bible says no drunkard will enter heaven."

She died, never having seen a change in Ralph. Ralph, due to his drinking, lived the last year of his life in the hospital. Forced sobriety brought about Ralph's ability to think about his relationship to God. Having experienced his mother's unfailing (unconditional) love, he could appreciate and did accept God's love for him in spite of the kind of person he was and the life he had lived.

It might have ended differently without anyone knowing about Ralph's conversion or without Ralph ever being converted. Nevertheless, who can deny that mother had biblical warrant for continuing to view her son as a child of God, one for whom Christ died, all the while warning him in the strongest possible terms (because they were spoken in love, not vindictively) that if he continued in his present unbelief and sin he would go the hell.

There was no reason for her to change her perspective, her mind-set, even when Ralph for 45 years appeared as complacent about his relationship to God as anyone could possibly be. Her view of Ralph as a child of God did not prevent her from warning Ralph about his persistent sin and indifference in the strongest possible terms!

Biblical Universalism is the God given warrant we have for viewing every sinner as "a child of God who is walking on the wrong path." We may not communicate the gospel on one basis to our children and on another basis to the unchurched. God is no respecter of persons.

Putting Premise B into Practice

This biblically warranted perspective does not dictate precisely *what* we ought to say to those we are trying to reach. That is determined by circumstances. Our perspective will, however, affect the way we say it and the attitude with which we will convey our message, whatever that message is.

The perspective of Biblical Universalism could be abused and so do great damage. That does not mean that we discard the premise, but rather that we search out the proper, effective, most beneficial and God glorifying way of using this perspective.

There is a concern that to say to an unbeliever "God loves you and Christ died for you" without adding a condition "if you believe," or "if you repent," that person will have no incentive to change his or her way of living. This concern is similar to the one raised against the doctrine of salvation by grace, that it "would make people indifferent or wicked."

Who can say that when the amazing truth of God's forgiving grace, freely and unconditionally given solely on the basis of Christ's merits, finally penetrated their heart and mind, that it made them careless or indifferent about God's will for their life? Why then should we hesitate to proclaim that good news unconditionally to others?

But what about the non-elect person to whom we might say "Christ died for you"? Underlying this seemingly insurmountable objection is the thought that we ought to say "Christ died for you," or any equivalent truth, only to those persons concerning whom we have absolute, unmistakable objective evidence that such is indeed the case. Such evidence or proof is never given to us!

The question is never whether we have objective knowledge of whether a particular person is one for whom Christ died. The only question is whether we have biblical warrant for assuming that such is the case. We can never get beyond **a biblically warranted assumption** (Pages 55, 56). This is the point of contact that the ambassador of Christ has with all those to whom he announces and declares the good news.

The Bible does not provide an answer for every question that can be raised concerning those who remain indifferent or who reject the witness of God in Christ. Here we encounter "the mystery of lawlessness." This is that area relating to "no man's land" (Page 43). The mystery of sin and unbelief poses questions which are safely and solemnly left in the hands of God.

All those for whom Christ died have the right to hear the unconditional good news of what God in Christ has done for them.

This is the gospel that will change their life, and the church has the responsibility to communicate that good news to them.

One can effectively, meaningfully and joyfully proclaim the gospel without differentiating or discriminating to all nations and to all people, only by proceeding on the biblically warranted assumption that all persons are elect in Christ except those who the Bible declares will be lost. The day of final judgment will reveal who the exceptions are among God's covenant people and among those outside the community of God's covenant people.

I have been pleasantly surprised by the number of missionaries from my own denomination as well as other Reformed Churches who have said that they always bring the good news on the assumption that those they approach with the gospel are persons for whom Christ died. They seem to sense that there can be no good news apart from this biblically warranted assumption (Chapter Nine). The biblical basis for this assumption, however, is seldom clearly articulated by them.

A Practical Question

Do we "respect ourselves as equal children of God and treat all other human beings with the same respect"? (See page 73.) Does the church have a problem with the way it views the unchurched? Is there a negativism about the approach that is often used in evangelism that hinders effective communication with "outsiders"?

Suppose you had a radio or TV ministry. Would you feel free to close your broadcasts by reciting the Lord's Prayer? Would you assume that the members of your audience were participants with you in praying "Our Father who art in heaven"? Or would you picture your listeners as spectators who for a moment are asked to listen to God's people pray? Would your hearers have the right to assume that you were including them in the "Our Father" since you had just been speaking to them? Would you, perhaps, conclude that it is inappropriate to use the Lord's Prayer, or any other prayer, in a radio or TV ministry?

Many worship services, both on radio and TV, switch to making announcements when the pastor leads the congregation in prayer. One wonders whether these broadcasters made this decision based upon the questions asked in the preceding paragraph. Do we feel free to identify ourselves with those to whom we communicate the gospel?

Messengers of the good news must identify themselves with those to whom they bring their message. They have biblical warrant for saying with Paul, "In Christ God was reconciling the world to himself, not counting their trespasses against them, and entrusting to us the message of reconciliation. So we are ambassadors for Christ, God making his appeal through us. We beseech you on behalf of Christ, be reconciled to God. For **our** sake he made him to be sin who knew no sin, so that in him **we** might become the righteousness of God" (2 Cor. 5:19-21, emphasis added).

When sinners remain indifferent to this good news, or harden themselves against it, God remains gracious as he, through his ambassadors, warns them to flee his wrath which is sure to come upon all who persist in unbelief and sin.

The message of missions is this: Christ died for **us** (you and me), and therefore **we** (you and I) must live for him.

Addendum A

[NOTE: The purpose of this addendum is to demonstrate that the premise developed in this book is consistent with the doctrine of the covenant, which is the basis for the practice of baptizing infants.]

The Church, The Covenant Community

The promise of the gospel together with the command to repent and believe "ought to be announced and declared *without differentiating or discriminating*, to all nations and people, to whom God in his good pleasure sends the gospel" (*Canons of Dort* II, 5, emphasis added). If the promise of the gospel and what it demands are to be declared to "all people" on the *same basis*, then what advantage or significance is there in being a member of the church?

The difference is not that all members of the church are born again Christians who are certain to be saved. There are hypocrites, pretenders, who are members of the church. All the more reason to ask, "What advantage does the church member have?"

In this addendum the church will be defined as all those who confess Jesus Christ as their Lord and Savior, and under the guidance of appointed officers, "meet together" (Heb. 10:25) for the purpose of worship, nurturing and instruction, according to the teachings of God's Word. This is sometimes called the visible church.

A church member is a member of the covenant community of God's people. To understand the advantage and significance of

111

being a member of the church, one must know what the Bible teaches about the covenant that God established with his people.

An Expressed Promise to Abraham and to His Descendants

A covenant, in the biblical sense of the word, is an oath-bound commitment or promise, usually accompanied with a sign. Scripture, unlike modern legal codes, knows nothing of an unexpressed, non-verbal, or implied covenant. This expressing, verbalizing (putting into words), clearly stating, belongs to **the essence** of the biblical idea of covenant.

Therefore, two distinct and *essential* elements are involved in God's covenant of grace. First of all there is the disposition or attitude of grace, that is, God's willingness to grant favor and blessing to those who are not deserving of his goodness. It is possible for God to have an attitude or disposition of grace toward sinners without having explicitly expressed or verbalized that attitude to them.

Secondly, there is the matter of making explicit, putting into words, expressing that attitude or disposition of grace to particular persons. God established his covenant of grace with Abraham and his descendants. God verbalized, expressed, made his promise explicit: "And I will establish my covenant between me and you and your descendants after you throughout their generations for an everlasting covenant, to be a God to you and to your descendants after you" (Gen. 17:7).

This covenant, established with Abraham and continued with his children, was sealed with the sign of circumcision: "You shall be circumcised in the flesh of your foreskins, and it shall be a sign of the covenant between me and you" (Gen. 17:11).

Ever since God established his covenant of grace with Abraham and his descendants, an externally identifiable community of people has continued to exist. They are God's covenant people. By God's commandment parents are permitted and required to express, reveal, verbalize God's promise of favor and blessing to their children from generation to generation.

Following Abraham, the covenant community consisted of Isaac and Jacob, whose descendants became the nation of Israel, the Old Testament (Old Covenant) people of God. God did wonderful things for them "such as have not been wrought in all the earth or in any nation" (Exod. 34:10). The Hebrews (The Jews, God's Old Testament [Old Covenant] people) could say "In many and various ways God spoke of old to our fathers by the prophets; but in these last days he has spoken to us by a Son" (Heb. 1:1).

Jesus the Mediator of the New Covenant

Through the ministry of Jesus Christ God continued to express reveal, make explicit his attitude of favor and grace. As the covenant continued in the New Testament (New Covenant) age, two significant changes were made.

First, the sign or seal of the covenant was changed. The original sign was that of circumcision—"He [Abraham] received circumcision as a sign or seal of the righteousness which he had by faith while he was still uncircumcised. The purpose was to make him the father of all who believe without being circumcised and who thus have righteousness reckoned to them" (Rom. 4:11).

Because Christ shed his blood once for all, the sign of God's attitude of favor and grace to undeserving sinners was changed to the non-bloody sign of baptizing with water. Water baptism became the "sign or seal of the righteousness" that God's people have by faith (grace). Both circumcision and baptism symbolize God's promise to remove the defilement of sin from his people.

Both of these covenant signs and seals declare what God promises to do by his grace. They are not a sign or seal of the covenant member's response to God's promise. The required response is to live as a child of God. Therefore the promise, as well as the sign of the promise, is appropriately given to those who are not old enough to immediately respond.

The second change that took place through the ministry of Jesus was that the declaring, verbalizing, expressing of God's attitude of blessing and grace was extended to the Gentiles as well as to the Jews. Gentiles who believe and their children with them are entitled to the sign of God's promise of grace when they are incorporated into the community of God's people, the church.

New Testament believers are the spiritual children of Abraham. Abraham is "the father of all who believe" (Rom. 4:11) because God first established his covenant (promise) of grace with Abraham. "I will bless you . . . so that you will be a blessing. . . and by you all the families of the earth shall be blessed" (Gen. 12:2,3).

Paul calls this promise "the gospel"—"And the scripture, foreseeing that God would justify the Gentiles by faith, preached *the gospel* beforehand to Abraham, saying 'In you shall all the nations be blessed.' So then, those who are men of faith are blessed with Abraham who had faith" (Gal. 3:8,9).

He redeemed us in order "that in Christ Jesus the blessing of Abraham might come upon the Gentiles" (Gal. 3:14). "If you are Christ's then are you Abraham's offspring, heirs according to the promise" (Gal. 3:29). Those who believe in the Lord Jesus Christ are the continuation of the covenant community of God's people initiated with the rite of circumcision. Therefore the Bible says, "For we are the true circumcision, who worship God in spirit, and glory in Christ Jesus" (Phil. 3:3). And again, "In him also you were circumcised with a circumcision made without hands, by putting off the body of flesh in the circumcision of Christ" (Col. 2:11).

There will always be a community of people to whom God reveals his attitude of favor and grace. Members of this covenant community receive baptism, the "sign or seal of the righteousness which [they have] by faith" (Rom. 4:11). God promises to be their God and the God of their children after them. Members of this covenant community must respond to this promise by living as those who belong to God.

If God's people persist in willful unbelief and sin they will not enjoy the blessings of the vow and promise given. "If at any time I declare concerning a nation or a kingdom that I will build and plant it, and if it does evil in my sight, not listening to my voice, then I will repent of the good which I had intended to do to it" (Jer. 18:9, 10).

To All Nations and People

The fact that God has a covenant community of people (the visible church) does not mean that his attitude or disposition of grace toward them is any different from his attitude toward the rest of mankind. It **does** mean that members of the church have God's promise revealed, verbalized, expressed to them with an oath and the sign or seal of that promise given to them.

The unsearchable riches of Christ were first expressed, revealed to the Jews as God's covenant people: "For I know the plans I have for you, says the Lord, plans for welfare and not for evil, to give you a future and hope" (Jer. 29:11); "Comfort, comfort my people says your God. Speak tenderly to Jerusalem, and cry to her that her warfare is ended, that her iniquity is pardoned" (Isa. 40:1).

Paul understood that through the coming of Christ he was permitted to declare "the unsearchable riches of Christ" to those outside the covenant community (the Gentiles) as well as to the Jews. This mystery "was not made known to the sons of men in other generations as it now has been revealed to his holy apostles and prophets by the Spirit; that is, how the Gentiles are fellow heirs, members of the same body, and partakers of the promise in Christ Jesus through the gospel" (Eph. 3:5, 6).

The situation was not that God had an attitude of indifference or hostility toward Gentiles before the mystery was revealed, and that through the coming of Christ this attitude toward the Gentiles was suddenly and drastically changed. Until the appointed time, the expression, verbalization, the special revelation of his forgiving grace "was not made known to the sons of men" (that is, those living outside God's covenant community of people). "The gentiles are fellow heirs, members of the same body."

Until God's appointed time the Gentiles were "strangers to the *covenants of promise*, having no hope and without God in the world" (Eph. 2:12, emphasis added). They were "strangers to" the expressed, explicit, verbalized "promise" and to the sign or seal of that promise. After Christ's death that which they had not known was to be "announced and declared" to all persons.

Because the **identical promise and demands** are to be declared to all people, the question with which we began this chapter remains. What advantage does the church member (the member of the covenant community) have? Paul anticipated this question when in Romans chapter two he spoke of the fact that what God promises and what he demands is **the same for all persons.**

We may substitute the word "baptism" for "circumcision" and the term "church member" for "Jew" as we read Romans 2:25-29, because the Jews were the covenant community of God's people. Therefore, if you are a member of the visible church:

> "[Baptism] indeed is of value if you obey the law; but if you break the law, your [baptism] becomes [unbaptism]. So, if a man who is [unbaptized] keeps the precepts of the

law, will not his [unbaptism] be regarded as [baptism]? Then those who are physically [unbaptized] but keep the law will condemn you who have the written code and [baptism] but break the law. For he is not a real [church member] who is one outwardly, nor is true [baptism] something external and physical. He is a [church member] who is one inwardly, and real [baptism] is a matter of the heart, spiritual and not literal. His praise is not from men but from God."

When a member of the church (the covenant community) disobeys God's will, he or she is judged for that disobedience just as the person who is not a member of the church is judged for disobedience to God's revealed will. If a non-church member keeps the precepts of the law, he or she is regarded just as the church member who keeps the law.

"The Very Words of God"

Paul continues: "Then what advantage has the [church member]? Or what is the value of [baptism]?" (Rom. 3:1). There appears to be no advantage. God treats all persons alike! Paul provides the answer: "Much in every way. To begin with, the [church members] are entrusted with the oracles of God" (Rom. 3:2).

The advantage of being a member of the covenant community (the visible church) is **not** that *only among them* is there salvation. The advantage is that they are entrusted with the "oracles of God," that is, the "very words of God" (Rom. 3:2, NIV). They are no longer "strangers to the covenants of [= characterized by] promise" (Eph. 2:12).

In baptism the very words of God are sealed with the sign of God's promise. Through baptism one is initiated into a community of people within which Christian faith can be nurtured, strengthened, and experienced in fellowship with others. Provision for such nurturing must follow baptism, whether it is adult or infant baptism. "And they devoted themselves to the apostle's teaching and fellowship, to breaking of bread and prayers" (Acts 2:42).

The advantage of such a sign and seal of the "very words of God," together with nurturing within the covenant community is beyond price. Its purpose is for all the members to help each member "attain to the unity of the faith and of the knowledge of the Son of God, to mature manhood, to the measure of the stature of the fullness of Christ" (Eph. 4:13).

In the New Testament we have the record of the gospel (the good news) being announced and declared beyond the covenant community for the first time. In such a setting the command is "Believe and be baptized!" in precisely that order. Whenever God's attitude of grace is announced and declared to those outside the church (outside the covenant community), those who hear are commanded to believe before they may receive the sign and seal of the promise of God's grace, namely baptism.

To Believers and Their Children

Upon believing, those persons and their children become members of the covenant community of God's people to whom God's promise of grace is given and are entitled to the sign and seal of God's promise of grace—"For the promise is to you and your children and to all that are far off, every one whom the Lord our God calls to him" (Acts 2:39).

This same pattern is seen today in those churches that practice infant baptism. In the established communities of God's covenant people, the baptism of adults occurs only occasionally. On the mission fields of these churches, where God's attitude of grace is being declared, announced, verbalized to those living outside the covenant community of God's people, adult baptisms and house-hold baptisms are a common occurrence. "She was baptized, with her household" (Acts 16:15).

A person is incorporated into God's covenant community of people either as a believer or as a child of a believer. In either case, if that person persistently and finally despises the expressed promise of God and neglects the nurture that in God's good providence was made available to him or her, their condemnation will be greater than if they had never been a member of the covenant community. "How much worse punishment do you think will be deserved by the man who has spurned the Son of God, and profaned the blood of the covenant by which he was sanctified, and outraged the Spirit of grace?" (Heb. 10:29).

The over-all message of Scripture is—All persons are elect in Christ except those who the Bible expressly declares will be finally lost (Premise B, Page 2). All persons (both those within and those outside God's covenant community of people) will enjoy God's favor and grace except those who willfully and finally refuse to live in obedience to God's will as it has been revealed to them (see Chapter Four).

God continues to express, verbalize his attitude of favor and grace, accompanied with a sign given to believers and their children, in order that from generation to generation the church may be "the pillar and bulwark of the truth," so that the mystery of our religion may be "preached among the nations, believed on in the world" (1 Tim. 3:15, 16).

ADDENDUM B

[Note: The following article appeared in *Mission Journal*, 8/87. It is used with permission and presents some challenging thoughts that are consistent with the premise developed in this book.]

For Whom Did Christ Die— and with What Result? A Modest Attempt At Bridgebuilding Between Calvinists and Arminians by Edward Fudge*

For about 400 years now, evangelical Christians have struggled to understand the meaning of Christ's death and the nature of the salvation he gives. How do we say Jesus died for "all"—and also that he came to save "the elect"? If Jesus died for "all," how can any be finally lost? Did Jesus save a nameless mass of people—or did he suffer for individuals with faces?

If the first option is correct, did Jesus' death actually *save* the people involved, or did it merely make salvation possible? If the second choice is biblical and Jesus died for specific men and

*Edward Fudge is an ordained minister and elder in the Churches of Christ. He is author of *The Fire That Consumes* (Providential Press 1982), a 500 page study of the doctrine of final punishment, and of *Our Man in Heaven*, a commentary on the book of Hebrews (Baker Book House, 1972). He holds B. A. and M. A. degrees in biblical languages from Abilene Christian University and the *Doctor Juris* from the University of Houston Law Center.

women, did that limit God's expansive love? Would such a "particular" atonement necessarily exclude anyone?

What of those who have never heard the gospel at all? Are they lost *because* they have not known of Jesus—something not their fault —or are they necessarily lost at all? If one suggests that they are not all lost, to what scriptural information might one point?

These are not questions with which Bible-believing evangelicals are unfamiliar. Neither are they questions with which we can refuse to seriously grapple. Calvinists and Arminians alike are paying them more than passing respect. In his apologetic treatise, *Reason Enough; A Case for the Christian Faith*, the Baptist scholar Clark H. Pinnock touches more than once on the function of non-Christian religions and the fate of those who have never heard the gospel. Pinnock writes from a Wesleyan/Arminian perspective ("freewill").

On the other hand, Christian Reformed pastor Neal Punt has generated considerable dialogue with his work *Unconditional Good News* (Wm. B. Eerdmans Pub. Co., 1980), and his smaller popular book, *What's Good About The Good News?*, is soon to appear. Punt holds to Calvinistic principles and presuppositions.

These are complex subjects and there are no easy answers to the intricate questions they raise. Some would say ordinary mortals should not waste time in search of solutions which have eluded the spiritual giants. Others believe we have no choice, and are convinced that God never intended for his people to remain divided forever on such fundamental issues as these.

I write as one reared in the Arminians' viewpoint, who then studied theology under Calvinists at Covenant Theological Seminary. At Covenant, I was viewed with suspicion as the lone Arminian in class. Since then, among those of my own heritage, I have often been suspect as a closet-Calvinist. The truth is, I do not believe either side has the whole truth packaged and labeled. Furthermore, no human system of thought ever will fully contain all the answers. God has simply not told us all we might wish to know, and whenever we pretend that he has, we find ourselves in a bed too short with covers too narrow.

On the other hand, there are likely thousands of us who come from reading the New Testament with a feeling that God has said more on these matters than we usually have. And we agree with the late Francis Schaeffer that we can speak truthfully, even when we cannot speak exhaustively. To that end—and with the strong conviction that Calvinists and Arminians can agree to a far greater extent than many in either camp have generally thought possible—I offer the seven couplets which follow as a modest attempt at bridgebuilding. This is only a beginning. But perhaps we can at least survey the terrain, establish some parameters, drive a few stakes. We certainly dare not simply shut our eyes and ears and continue shouting ancient arguments which often miss everybody's points.

COUPLET 1:

Every person deserves to be lost.

No person deserves to be saved.

The apostle Paul put it this way: "All . . . are under the power of sin, as it is written . . . that every mouth may be stopped, and the whole world may be held accountable to God" (Rom. 3:9-19). "For there is no distinction, since all have sinned and fall short of the glory of God" (Rom. 3:23).

God demands absolute holiness and not one of us has presented it. From this point of view, the mystery is not that some are finally lost but that anyone is finally saved. Whoever takes seriously the radical demands of God's character quickly acknowledges his or her own sin.

This means that every person finally lost receives justice, whereas every person finally saved receives mercy which is not deserved. It also means that every person finally lost must accept all the blame, but that every person finally saved must give God all the credit. There is no injustice with God (Rom. 3:4-8). His judgment of wrath will be right—as even the lost will confess (Rom. 1:18-20, 32; 2:5).

There are genuine and important differences between Augustine and Pelagius, between Calvin and Arminius. But here there need be no controversy. Every careful Calvinist insists that God deserves no blame for the lost, and every advocate of free will familiar with the biblical text knows that God deserves all the credit for the salvation of the saved. If each side had stressed those points, their differences would have been focused more sharply, misunderstandings would have been minimized, and all Christians would have been richer as a result.

COUPLET 2:

God takes no pleasure in the final destruction of any person.

God would find pleasure in every person being saved.

This couplet merely paraphrases the New Testament language. "God . . . desires all men to be saved and to come to the knowledge of the truth" (1 Tim. 2:4). He is "not wishing that any should perish . . . " (2 Pet. 3:9).

Again, there is no necessary conflict between Calvinist and Arminian. Whatever God's eternal purpose includes, God tells us plainly in Scripture that he is not vengeful or vindictive. God does not delight in the destruction of any person he has made—even his enemies. Whoever is lost will not see God smiling as a result.

COUPLET 3:

No one can come to Jesus unless the Father draws that one.

Every person whom the Father has given to Jesus will come to him.

These statements did not originate with John Calvin, Saint Augustine or even the Apostle Paul, but with the Lord Jesus Christ himself (John 6:37, 44). Far from being an obstacle to world mission, these truths provide its greatest incentive and only solid basis. If God has no over-arching purpose which he is certain to fulfill, if the salvation of mankind depends ultimately on the obedience and skill and efforts and success of other humans, then evangelism stands on shaky ground indeed. It is the conviction that God has a plan—and a people —which empowers us to proclaim the good news that Jesus died for sinners (Acts 18:9-10). This assurance constantly reminds us that what God began in eternity he will bring unfailingly to fruition in the course of time (Eph. 1:1-14; Rom. 8:28-31).

If the thought of election troubles us, as though God's choice of some requires his rejection of others (what is known in some circles as "double predestination"), we may simply rejoice that here Scripture is "splendidly illogical," to borrow words from A.

M. Hunter. For, as Hunter notes, "the opposite of election is not predestination to destruction; it is unbelief—a self-incurred thing" (*The Gospel According to St. Paul*, Westminster, 1966). Numerous Reformed writers have stressed the same point—which Arminians of course have happily received.

We must catch this vision of divine sovereignty if we are to find our own place in God's purposeful plan. In these days of self-help schemes and positive-attitude platitudes, the Reformation's clarion call of sovereign grace spotlights the shallowness of much contemporary preaching. It provides a message that still can revolutionize the church and turn the world upside down.

This message of the divine initiative in salvation smites our own pride even while it ignites holy courage. None can come to Jesus—despite our clever phrases, latest methods and most effective salesmanship —unless the Father draws that one. On the other hand, every person the Father has given to Jesus will come to him—without exception, and despite our own inadequacies, disobedience or bumbling efforts. If prophets are mute, donkeys can talk. If we are silent, the stones can cry out. But if that happens, though God's plan will go on, we will be called to account for our own disobedience.

COUPLET 4:

Every person finally lost will be lost on the basis of his or her own works.

Every person finally saved will be saved on the basis of Jesus' work.

In some sense, God is "Savior of all," though "especially" of those who believe (I Tim. 4:10). At the same time, many New Testament texts indicate that not every human being finally will be saved.

On the other hand, the Bible leaves no doubt that every person finally saved will enjoy salvation only because of what God did in Jesus Christ. Christians may therefore believe, and should always make plain, that (whatever else may be said or unsaid) the manifest basis on which God will bestow resurrection immortality to every person who inherits it will be the atonement accomplished at Golgotha and attested to by the empty tomb.

"No one comes to the Father," said Jesus, "but by me" (John 14:6). "There is salvation in no one else" (Acts 4:12). All who "receive the abundance of grace and the free gift of righteousness" will do so "through the one man Jesus Christ" (Rom. 5:17). It is the "act of righteousness" of the "one man" Jesus Christ that "leads to acquittal and life" for all who finally are saved (Rom. 5:18).

In these matters, there is no difference between those who lived prior to Jesus' birth and after it—or between Jew and Gentile—or between those who have known of Jesus and those who have not. None will be saved except on the basis of Jesus' atonement. Salvation will be exclusively "to the praise of his glory" (Eph. 1:6, 12, 14). Throughout the ages to come, every redeemed human being will be a trophy to "the immeasurable riches of his grace" (Eph. 2:7). And every person who perishes finally in hell will do so despite the fact that Jesus died for sinners and despite the fact that none who comes to him is ever turned away.

COUPLET 5:

Salvation, considered objectively, was accomplished almost 2,000 years ago in the work of Jesus Christ on the earth.

Salvation, considered subjectively, begins when each individual responds in trust to God's gracious call.

Jesus himself announced that he came "to save the lost" or "to save the world" (Luke 19:10; John 12:47). In short, he came "to save sinners" (1 Tim. 1:15). Jesus accomplished what he came to do, and on the cross he proclaimed, "It is finished" (John 19:30). God himself saw the finished work of atonement and was satisfied (Isa. 53:11). Because Jesus had justified those he came to save, he did not remain dead, but was raised up on the third day (Rom. 4:25). Because he had accomplished purification for sins, he took his place at God's right hand (Heb. 1:3; 10:11-14).

All this occurred then, during the earthly ministry of Jesus our substitute and Savior. God was reconciling the world to himself "in Christ," that is, in Jesus' fleshly body, during the days of the Son's humiliation (2 Cor. 5:18-19; Col: 1:19-22).

In a very real sense, therefore, the gospel is "the good news of our salvation" (Eph. 1:13). It proclaims not salvation's possibility but its accomplishment. First God saved us. Then he called us with the holy gospel to respond to what he had done (2 Tim. 1:9-10). We speak of this finished aspect of Christ's work as *objective* salvation. It happened once for all, outside of us but for us, in the personal doing and dying of Jesus of Nazareth.

At the same time, every person who enjoys salvation in this life does so by a response of faith to God's gracious call. Whatever the case may be in the world to come, no one can enjoy salvation in this life apart from such a response of faith. Furthermore, since that weekend almost 2,000 years ago when Jesus died and rose again, no person can fully enjoy salvation in this life apart from hearing and believing the gospel.

Just as President Lincoln signed the Emancipation Proclamation and, by the stroke of a pen, objectively freed every Black American slave, so Jesus Christ, by his obedience in life and unto death, objectively saved every human being who finally will be saved. And just as no American slave personally enjoyed the benefits of Lincoln's act until he or she heard and believed the good news of emancipation, so no redeemed sinner *subjectively* enjoys Christ's redemption now except through the preaching and belief of the gospel. In this sense, we are presently "being saved" (1 Cor. 1:18; Acts 16:31; Rom. 10:9).

Until men and women learn the good news of their salvation, they continue to live as if nothing had happened. They remain as they had been—without hope, not knowing God, unaware of his forgiveness and favor. The gospel ministry is for the sake of such men and women —that they may obtain salvation, subjectively as well as objectively (2 Tim. 2:10). Like Paul at ancient Corinth, we also need to declare the gospel fearlessly and without ceasing, for God still has many people who have not yet heard the good news of what he has done for them in Jesus (Acts 18:9-10; 2 Cor. 5:18-19; 2 Pet. 3:9).

COUPLET 6:

Every person finally lost will have rejected relationship and fellowship with God, however it was presented to him or her.

Every person finally saved will have accepted relation-ship and fellowship with God, however it was presented to him or her.

Scripture speaks of some who perish for lack of knowledge, but two things need to be said. Such "knowledge" refers to relationship with God rather than mere intellectual information. And such people have rejected that "knowledge" by their own conscious choice (Hosea 4:6; 2 Thess. 2:10-12). To intentionally reject God's light spells condemnation (John 3:19). Apart from some such rejection, no individual will finally be lost, so great is the saving work Jesus accomplished (Rom. 5:13-14, 18-21).

Yet not all who are finally lost will have rejected the gospel, for not all will have heard it, at least in this life. But all who are finally lost will have rejected God's "knowledge" in some form, whether it came to them in nature (Acts 14:17; Rom. 1:19-25), conscience (Rom. 2:15-16), or the Old Testament Scriptures (Rom. 2:12; John 5:45-47). God's judgment against those finally lost will be manifestly just (Rom. 2:5-12).

On the other hand, just as every person finally saved will be saved on the basis of the work Jesus accomplished, so every person finally saved apparently will have responded in a spirit of faith to God's gracious beckon. Paul applies this principle to those who lived and died in years B.C. as well as to those who lived in years A.D. The same principle applies to Gentile as well as to Jew. "God is one, and he will justify the circumcised on the ground of their faith and the uncircumcised because of their faith" (Rom. 3:30).

Abraham offers the prime example of this, for before his circumcision he was pre-Jew as well as pre-Christian. Even Abraham was justified by faith, though the content of his gospel understanding was limited indeed (Rom. 4:9-22).

Those who never hear the gospel and are finally lost will have rejected relationship and fellowship with God in the way it was offered to them. Those who never hear the gospel and are finally saved will be saved because of what Jesus did on behalf of sinners, even though they never heard about it; but they will also be people of whom it may be said that they trusted God's grace which was presented to them.

In this respect the case is the same with those who have heard the gospel. Those who hear the gospel and are saved will have trusted God's ultimate word of grace in the gospel. Those who hear the gospel and are finally lost will have rejected God's ultimate word of grace in the gospel. Jesus was speaking of those who hear the gospel when he said: "He who believes and is baptized will be saved; but he who does not believe will be condemned" (Mark 16:16).

COUPLET 7:

No person is better for remaining ignorant of the gospel.

No person is injured by hearing the gospel.

Sometimes people mistakenly assume, upon learning that Jesus' work saves all who are finally saved whether they heard the gospel or not, that those who never hear are somehow better off by remaining in that condition. Nothing could be farther from the truth.

It is true that ultimately rejection of God is the rejection of his brightest light and fullest revelation of grace in the gospel. For that reason, it is also true that whoever willfully rejects the gospel deserves the greatest punishment possible (Heb. 6:6; 10:26-31). But it does not therefore follow that any person will reject the brightest light who previously consistently accepted God's dimmer rays. The heart of each individual remains the same regardless of the degree of light to which it is exposed.

Whoever rejected the law and the prophets would not believe even if one should rise from the dead, said our Lord (Luke 16:30-31). Even the unsealed prophecy of the Apocalypse does not change the hearts of those who hear its message. The evildoers do evil still, the filthy remain in their filth, the righteous continue to do right, and the holy are holy still (Rev. 22:11).

The subjective enjoyment of salvation in this life depends on hearing the gospel and believing it. On the other hand, no person who rejects the gospel and is finally lost would have been saved had he or she never heard of Jesus, for it is unthinkable that anyone whose heart cried "Yes" to God from the hopeless darkness could suddenly shout a defiant "No" when the Cross and Empty Tomb finally burst into view.

Finally . . .

These seven couplets are neither Calvinistic nor Arminian. They are biblical propositions which transcend both points of view. These affirmations may be proclaimed with conviction by all Christians, although they fit neatly into the tidy mental boxes of no established school of thought in particular. They provide a starting point for a closer walk together and a clearer understanding of God's Word, modest as that beginning point might be.

Finally, all this is encapsulated best in words found in the Gospel According to John, beginning with what probably is the best-known and most-loved verse of the Bible:

> God so loved the world that he gave his only Son, that whoever believes in him should not perish but have eternal life. For God sent the Son into the world, not to condemn the world, but that the world might be saved through him. He who believes in him is not condemned; he who does not believe is condemned already, because he has not believed in the name of the only Son of God. And this is the judgment, that the light has come into the world, and men loved darkness rather than light, because their deeds were evil. For everyone who does evil hates the light, and does not come to the light, lest his deeds should be exposed. But he who does what is true comes to the light, that it may be clearly seen that his deeds have been wrought in God (John 3:16-21).

Glossary

Absolute Universalism - The teaching that all persons will be finally saved. God's judgment against sin is temporary, designed to make sinners flee from sin, hate evil and recognize Christ as their Savior.

Arminianism, five declarations of - See Canons of Dort.

Atonement - The satisfaction of God's justice made by Jesus Christ which was necessary for the forgiveness of sinners.

Augustinianism - The teaching that all persons are outside of Christ except those whom God in his sovereign, incomprehensible love has chosen to bring to salvation.

Baptism - The dipping in or sprinkling with water in the name of the triune God as the New Testament sign or seal of God's promise of Grace.

Belgic Confession - One of the confessions of the Reformed Churches. It consists of 37 Articles and was written in 1561.

Biblical Universalism - The teaching that all persons are elect in Christ and will surely come to salvation except those who the Bible expressly declares will be finally lost.

Calvinism's five responses to Arminianism - See Canons of Dort.

Canons of Dort - Five doctrinal statements adopted by the Reformed Churches in 1619 in response to the teachings of Arminianism. These statements seek to refute the Arminian teachings of conditional election, universal atonement, partial depravity, resistible grace and the possibility of lapsing from grace.

Church - See Visible Church

Circumcision - The Old Testament sign or seal of the covenant of grace established with Abram. It was a bloody sign consisting of the removal of the foreskin of the male organ, symbolizing true circumcision which is the removal of sin from the heart and life of God's people.

Condemnation - The final judgment of eternal death as punishment for sin.

Covenant - An expressed, verbalized commitment or promise usually accompanied with a sign.

Covenant community of God's people - See the Visible Church.

Covenant of grace - God's expressed commitment or promise of his attitude of grace. Accompanied in the Old Testament with the sign of circumcision and in the New Testament with the sign of baptism.

Election - The teaching that God in Christ has unconditionally chosen his people to salvation.

Faith - A knowledge of and confidence in the truth of God's Word.

Generalization - A declaration or statement which is generally true or valid even though there may be exceptions to it.

Gospel demands - Appeals to ethical conduct which are based on the assumption that the person addressed is a new creature in Christ. These are summarized in the familiar trio—repent, believe, obey.

Grace - God's goodness or favor to those who are undeserving.

Immediate imputation - The teaching that the sin of Adam and/or the righteousness of Christ are accounted to those persons represented by Adam and Christ without any self-determined act on the part of the persons so represented.

Justification - God's act of declaring his people righteous on the basis of Christ's sacrifice and perfect obedience offered in their behalf.

Mediator - The role Christ took upon himself in reconciling sinners to God.

Moralism - The teaching that our good works earn our acceptance by God.

New Covenant - The form of the covenant of grace found in the New Testament (New Covenant) as it is extended to people throughout the world accompanied with the sign of baptism.

Old Covenant - The form of the covenant of grace found in the Old Testament (Old Covenant) established primarily with the Jewish nation accompanied with the sign of circumcision.

Original sin - The corrupt nature with which all the descendants of Adam (except Jesus Christ) are born as a result of the disobedience of Adam and Eve in Paradise.

Pelagianism - The teaching that all persons are lost except those who by their own strength and will lead a good life, following the example of Christ.

Penitence - A heart-felt sorrow for sin.

Premise A - All persons are outside of Christ (that is "lost, "condemned, "on the way to hell, "under law, "children of wrath) except those who the Bible expressly declares will be saved.

Premise B - All persons are elect in Christ (that is "will be saved, "justified, "on the way to heaven, "under grace, "children of God) except those who the Bible expressly declares will be finally lost.

Propitiation - The act of God in turning away his wrath against sin for the sake of Christ's sacrifice.

Qualified Universalism - See Biblical Universalism

Reconciliation - The act of God in Christ re-establishing sinners in a right relationship to himself for the sake of Christ's merits.

Redemption - The act of God by which he delivers sinners from the consequences of their sin by the ransom paid by Christ on the cross.

Regeneration - The giving of new life by the Holy Spirit to those who were spiritually dead, also called New Birth.

Repentance - A sincere sorrow for sin and turning to God as Savior and Lord.

Reprobation - The teaching that only those who, in addition to their sin in Adam, willfully, stubbornly and finally persist in unbelief and sin will experience God's sentence of eternal death.

Semi-Pelagianism - The teaching that all persons are lost except those who by their sovereign decision accept God's gracious offer of salvation.

Special Revelation - The truth declared by God in the Bible.

Universalism - See Absolute Universalism, Biblical Universalism

Universal - A declaration or statement which is true or valid in every instance with no exceptions.

Visible Church - All those persons who confess Jesus Christ as Lord and Savior, who gather for worship, nurturing, and instruction according to the teachings of God's Word.

Subject Index

Textual Index

WHAT'S GOOD ABOUT THE GOOD NEWS?

Published by – Northland Press
P.O. Box 42756, Chicago, IL 60642
Cover Design – John deVries
Text Design and Typography – Amy Nelson
Set in Linotype Times Roman
Typesetting, Printing and Binding –
TypeMart Corp., P.O. Box 8, Lansing, IL 60438